HEROES

21 True Stories of Courage and Honor—With Exercises for Developing Critical Reading Skills

Henry Billings
Melissa Billings

Jamestown Publishers
Providence, Rhode Island

HEROES
21 True Stories of Courage and Honor—With
Exercises for Developing Critical Reading Skills

Catalog No. 764
Copyright ©1985 by Jamestown Publishers

Cover Illustration by Bob Eggleton
Cover and Text Design by Deborah Hulsey Christie

Printed in the United States   DP

91 92 93 94 95 12 11 10 9 8 7 6

ISBN 0-89061-450-4

Contents

GROUP THREE

To the Teacher

INTRODUCTION

Most young people develop heroes—people whose actions or beliefs they admire and strive to emulate. They might meet those admirable figures in literature, in the news, in the movies, in their own neighborhoods, or on the playing fields of their favorite sports. Heroes provide models for growth . . . for personal development. They affect ideals and behavior. Consequently, they are of great importance.

Heroes presents an array of heroic figures, including explorers, political idealists, humanitarians, social reformers, sports personalities, and the person next door. They are men and women, young and old. They span cultures and time. They embody the truth that heroes are not born but are created by the most dangerous and trying circumstances of life. Heroes are individuals who exhibit extraordinary physical, mental or spiritual courage. And the seed of heroism lies in every one of us.

Heroes provides subject matter for thoughtful interpretation and discussion, while challenging your students in four critical reading categories: main idea, important details, inferences, and vocabulary in context. *Heroes* can also help your students to improve their reading rates. Timing of the selections is optional, but many teachers find it an effective motivating device.

Heroes consists of twenty-one units divided into three groups of seven units each. All the stories in a group are on the same reading level. Group One is at the sixth-grade reading level, Group Two at the seventh, and Group Three at the eighth, as assessed by the Fry Formula for Estimating Readability.

HOW TO USE THIS BOOK

Introducing the Book. This text, used creatively, can be an effective tool for learning certain critical reading skills. We suggest that you begin by introducing the students to the contents and format of the book. Examine the book with the students to see how it is set up and what it is about. Discuss the title. What is a *hero*? (Try to develop the idea that there are all kinds of heroes. Some fight physically for what they believe, sometimes getting injured or dying in the process. Some speak out publicly for their ideals, trying to bring about change through peaceful means. Some struggle against the difficult and the dangerous to open up new possibilities, new frontiers. All struggle to overcome some great difficulty—they give everything they've got. The situations that call up heroism are as diverse as life itself.) Read through the table of contents as a class, to gain an overview of the heroes who will be encountered.

The Sample Unit. To learn what is contained in each unit and how to proceed through a unit, turn to the Sample Unit on pages 10–15. After you have examined these pages yourself, work through the Sample Unit with your students, so that they may have a clear understanding of the purpose of the book and of how they are to use it.

The Sample Unit is set up exactly as the regular units are. At the beginning there is a photograph or illustration accompanied by a brief introduction to the story. The story is next, followed by four types of comprehension exercises: Finding the Main Idea, Recalling Facts, Making Inferences, and Using Words Precisely.

Begin by having someone in the class read aloud the introduction that appears with the picture. Then give the students a few moments to study the picture. Ask for their thoughts on what the story will be about. Continue the discussion for a minute or so. Then have the students read the story. (You may wish to time the students' reading, in order to help them improve their reading speed as well as their comprehension. A Words per Minute table is located in the back of the book, to help the students figure their reading rates.)

Then go through the sample questions as a class. An explanation of the comprehension skill and directions for answering the questions are given at the beginning of each exercise. Make sure all the students understand how to answer the four different types of questions and how to figure their scores. The correct answers and sample scores are printed in lighter type. Also, explanations of all the correct answers are given within the sample Main Idea and Making Inferences exercises, to help the students understand how to think through these question types.

As the students are working their way through the Sample Unit, be sure to have them turn to the Words per Minute table on pages 154 and 155 (if you have timed their reading) and the Reading Speed and Critical Reading Scores graphs on pages 156 and 157 at the appropriate points. Explain to the students the purpose of each, and read the directions with them. Be sure they understand how the table and graphs will be used. You will probably have to help them find and mark their scores for the first unit or two.

Timing the Story. If you are going to time your students' reading, explain to them your reason for doing so: to help them keep track of and improve their reading rates.

Here's one way of timing. Have all the students in the class begin reading the story at the same time. After one minute has passed, write on the chalkboard the time that has elapsed, and begin updating it at ten-second intervals (1:00, 1:10, 1:20, etc.). Tell the students to copy down the last time shown on the chalkboard when they have finished reading. They should write their reading time in the space designated after the story.

Have the students check their reading rates by using the Words per Minute table on pages 154 and 155. They should then enter their reading speed on the Reading Speed graph on page

156. Graphing their reading rates allows the students to keep track of improvement in their reading speed.

Working Through Each Unit. If the students have carefully completed all parts of the Sample Unit, they should be ready to tackle the regular units. In each unit, begin by having someone in the class read aloud the introduction to the story, just as you did in the Sample Unit. Discuss the topic of the story, and allow the students time to study the illustration.

Then have the students read the story. If you are timing them, have the students enter their reading time, find their reading speed, and record their speed on the graph after they have finished reading the story.

Next, direct the students to complete the four comprehension exercises *without* looking back at the story. When they have finished, go over the questions and answers with them. The students will grade their own answers and make the necessary corrections. They should then enter their Critical Reading Scores on the graph on page 157.

The Graphs. Students enjoy graphing their work. Graphs show, in a concrete and easily understandable way, how a student is progressing. Seeing a line of progressively rising scores gives students the incentive to continue to strive for improvement.

Check the graphs regularly. This will allow you to establish a routine for reviewing each student's progress. Discuss with each student what the graphs show and what kind of progress you expect. Establish guidelines and warning signals so that students will know when to approach you for counseling and advice.

RELATED TEXTS

If you find that your students enjoy and benefit from the stories and skills exercises in *Heroes*, you may be interested in *Disasters!*, *Phenomena*, and *Monsters*, three related Jamestown texts. All feature high-interest stories and work in four critical reading comprehension skills. As in *Heroes*, the units in those books are divided into three groups, at reading levels six, seven and eight.

The man pictured above was an ordinary passenger on an ordinary flight out of National Airport in Washington, D.C. But he never made it to his destination. Instead, he found himself struggling for his life in the icy waters of the Potomac River. And in those frigid waters, Arland Williams became a hero.

The Man in the Water

On January 13, 1982, a severe snowstorm hit Washington, D.C. The temperature fell to the mid teens. Driving snow made it hard to see. Flights out of Washington's National Airport were delayed while snowplows cleared the runways. Air Florida Flight 90, with its seventy-nine passengers, was no exception. It was originally scheduled to depart at 2:15 P.M. Clearing the runways, however, took over an hour. At 3:37, the pilot was finally allowed to move the plane into position for takeoff. But fifteen other planes were lined up ahead of it. Another twenty minutes went by before Flight 90 could roll out onto the runway.

While Flight 90 was waiting for the runways to be plowed, the ice that had formed on its wings was removed. But new ice began to form immediately. As the pilot waited for the fifteen other planes to take off, the ice grew heavier. An ice buildup on a plane's wings is dangerous. It makes the plane heavier and disturbs the normal flow of air over the wings. Despite the fresh layer of ice, Flight 90 roared down the runway when its turn came at 3:59 P.M.

As the jet took off, it shuddered. Something was wrong. It was not gaining altitude as it should. One of the passengers, who was also a pilot, said, "We're not going to make it."

Meanwhile, traffic on the Fourteenth Street Bridge over the Potomac River was heavy. It was rush hour, and workers who lived outside the city were headed home. Suddenly the blue, green and white form of an Air Florida 727 appeared out of the clouds. Flight 90 was going down, and it was heading straight for the crowded bridge. The motorists on the bridge could do nothing but watch in horror as the airplane fell from the sky and smashed across the northbound lane. The tops of several cars were sheared off. Four motorists were killed before the plane plunged into the frigid Potomac and broke in two.

Rescue workers arrived on the scene quickly. Their searchlights revealed a hideous sight. Many of the passengers could be seen still strapped in their seats at the bottom of the Potomac. Only six passengers were still alive. They clung to a piece of the tail section that stuck out of the water. One of the people was a balding man with a large mustache. He seemed to be more alert and less severely injured than any of the others.

Speed was essential if the six people were to be saved. A person can last only a few minutes in such cold water. The rescue was made difficult by the fact that there was only enough room for one helicopter to get between the Fourteenth Street Bridge and another bridge nearby.

A rescue helicopter arrived and quickly lowered its lifeline and flotation ring to the balding man. The man grabbed it, but instead of using it himself, he passed it on to one of the other passengers. As that person was lifted out of the freezing water, the balding man fought to keep his grip on the tail section. His body temperature was dropping, and the numbing cold of the water was sapping his strength. When the rescue helicopter returned, the lifeline was again dropped to him. Bystanders watched in amazement as the man once again passed the lifeline on to someone else. For the second time, he was giving up a chance to save himself in order to allow another person to be saved.

After a nerve-racking ten minutes, the three other passengers had been taken safely to the shore. Only the balding man was left in the river. But when the helicopter returned to pick him up, he was gone. He had been in the icy water too long.

For several days, the selfless hero was known simply as "the man in the water." No one knew who he was. But when the passenger list was compared with the description of the man, it was determined that he was Arland Williams, a forty-six-year-old bank examiner from Atlanta, Georgia.

When Arland Williams boarded Flight 90, he was an ordinary person on an ordinary flight. There was nothing special about him. Even his mother described him as "just average." He was simply another face in the crowd.

Like anyone else, Arland Williams wanted to live. In fact, he always insisted on sitting in the back of the plane "because it's safer back there." But at 4:01 P.M. on a stormy January day, when the plane he was on slammed into a bridge and tumbled into the Potomac, Williams chose to risk his life to save the lives of others. We don't know what he was thinking when he found himself hanging on to the tail section of that broken airplane. But he must have known that the longer he stayed in the water the more certain it was that he would die. Yet he did stay in the cold, black water and pass his lifeline on to others.

The "man in the water" became a national hero. He had given up his life so that other people might live. ■

If you have been timed while reading this selection, enter your reading time below. Then turn to the Words per Minute table on page 154 and look up your reading speed (words per minute). When you are working through the regular units, you will then enter your reading speed on the graph on page 156.

REACING TIME: Sample Unit

_____ : _____
Minutes   Seconds

How well did you read?

- *The four types of questions that follow appear in each unit in this book. The directions for each kind of question tell you how to mark your answers. In this Sample Unit, the answers are marked for you. Also, for the Main Idea and Making Inferences exercises, explanations of the answers are given, to help you understand how to think through these question types. Read through these exercises carefully.*

- *When you have finished all four exercises in a unit, you will check your work by using the answer key that starts on page 150. For each right answer, you will put a check mark (✔) on the line beside the box. For each wrong answer, you will write the correct answer on the line.*

- *For scoring each exercise, you will follow the directions below the questions. In this unit, sample scores are entered as examples.*

A FINDING THE MAIN IDEA

Look at the three statements below. One expresses the main idea of the story you just read. A good main idea statement answers two questions: it tells *who* or *what* is the subject of the story, and it answers the understood question *does what?* or *is what?* Another statement is *too broad*, it is vague and doesn't tell much about the topic of the story. The third statement is *too narrow*, it tells about only one part of the story.

Match the statements with the three answer choices below by writing the letter of each answer in the box in front of the statement it goes with.

M—Main Idea   **B—Too Broad**   **N—Too Narrow**

✔ [M] 1. Arland Williams, an average person, became a hero when he died in the Potomac River because he twice passed his lifeline on to save others.
[This is the *main idea*. It tells who the story is about and what he did.]

✔ [N] 2. Arland Williams died in the icy Potomac River after the plane he was on crashed on takeoff.
[This statement is *too narrow*. It doesn't tell anything about Williams's heroism.]

✔ [B] 3. A bank examiner from Georgia became a hero when he died by putting the lives of others ahead of his own.
[This statement is true, but it is *too broad*. It doesn't tell who the man was or exactly what he did.]

15 Score 15 points for a correct *M* answer
10 Score 5 points for each correct *B* or *N* answer
25 TOTAL SCORE: Finding the Main Idea

B RECALLING FACTS

How well do you remember the facts in the story you just read? Put an x in the box in front of the correct answer to each of the multiple-choice questions below.

1. The plane crash took place in
   - ___ ☐ a. Florida.
   - ___ ☐ b. Atlanta.
   - ✓ ☒ c. Washington, D.C.

2. Air Florida Flight 90 crashed into the Potomac River
   - ✓ ☒ a. right after takeoff.
   - ___ ☐ b. thirty minutes after takeoff.
   - ___ ☐ c. as it was attempting to land.

3. Immediately after the crash, there were only
   - ___ ☐ a. two passengers alive.
   - ✓ ☒ b. six passengers alive.
   - ___ ☐ c. five passengers alive.

4. Arland Williams died because he
   - ___ ☐ a. had suffered head injuries in the crash.
   - ___ ☐ b. did not know how to swim.
   - ✓ ☒ c. had been in the icy water too long.

5. Arland Williams always insisted on sitting
   - ✓ ☒ a. in the back of the plane.
   - ___ ☐ b. near the exit doors.
   - ___ ☐ c. in the front of the plane.

Score 5 points for each correct answer

__25__ TOTAL SCORE: Recalling Facts

C MAKING INFERENCES

An inference is a judgment that is made or an idea that is arrived at based on facts or on information that is given. You make an inference when you understand something that is *not* stated directly, but that is *implied*, or suggested by the facts that are given.

Below are five statements that are judgments or ideas that have been arrived at from the facts of the story. Write the letter *C* in the box in front of each statement that is a correct inference. Write the letter *F* in front of each faulty inference.

C—Correct Inference   F—Faulty Inference

✓ C 1. The crash of Air Florida Flight 90 was caused, at least in part, by the delayed takeoff.

[This is a *correct* inference. Waiting in line for the other planes to take off allowed the ice to build up again on the wings.]

✓ F 2. If the rescue workers had arrived on the scene sooner, most of the seventy-nine passengers could have been saved.

[This is a *faulty* inference. The rescue workers did arrive quickly. Most of the passengers died on impact or within just a minute or two.]

✓ C 3. If two helicopters had been able to operate at the scene of the crash, Arland Williams would have been saved.

[This is a *correct* inference. If one helicopter could save five out of six, then two helicopters would probably have been able to rescue all six.]

✓ F 4. Arland Williams's job prepared him to handle such an emergency.

[This is a *faulty* inference. He was a bank examiner, not a rescue worker.]

✓ F 5. Arland Williams had always wanted to be a hero.

[This is a *faulty* inference. Before the crash, Arland Williams was an ordinary person. He did not go out of his way to seek danger.]

Score 5 points for each correct answer

__25__ TOTAL SCORE: Making Inferences

D USING WORDS PRECISELY

Each of the numbered sentences below contains an underlined word or phrase from the story you have just read. Under the sentence are three definitions. One has the *same* meaning as the underlined word or phrase, one has *almost the same* meaning, and one has the *opposite* meaning. Match the definitions with the three answer choices by writing the letter that stands for each answer in the box in front of the definition it goes with.

S—Same   A—Almost the Same   O—Opposite

1. Despite the fresh layer of ice, Flight 90 roared down the runway when its turn came at 3:59 P.M.

✓ [S] a. in spite of
✓ [A] b. although
✓ [O] c. because of

2. Their searchlights revealed a hideous sight.

✓ [A] a. upsetting
✓ [O] b. pleasant
✓ [S] c. ghastly

3. Speed was essential if the six people were to be saved.

✓ [A] a. important
✓ [S] b. necessary
✓ [O] c. unneeded

4. His body temperature was dropping, and the numbing cold of the water was sapping his strength.

✓ [O] a. restoring
✓ [S] b. draining
✓ [A] c. using

5. But when the passenger list was compared with the description of the man, it was determined that he was Arland Williams, a forty-six-year-old bank examiner from Atlanta, Georgia.

✓ [O] a. remained uncertain
✓ [A] b. decided
✓ [S] c. found

__15__ Score 3 points for each correct *S* answer
__10__ Score 1 point for each correct *A* or *O* answer

__25__ TOTAL SCORE: Using Words Precisely

● *Enter the four total scores in the spaces below, and add them together to find your Critical Reading Score. Then record your Critical Reading Score on the graph on page 157.*

_____	Finding the Main Idea
_____	Recalling Facts
_____	Making Inferences
_____	Using Words Precisely
_____	CRITICAL READING SCORE: Sample Unit

To the Student

Almost everyone has heroes—people they look up to and perhaps try to imitate in some way. There are all kinds of heroes. Some use their physical strength or power to help others or to make great discoveries. Some use the power of words. Some work to set a good example for others to follow. Some just give everything they have to give for a cause they believe in. What they all have in common is great courage—the desire and the determination to work for something they believe in deeply, even in the face of great odds. *Heroes* brings you the stories of twenty-one people who made a difference in the world through their courageous actions.

While you are enjoying these inspiring stories, you will be developing your reading skills. This book assumes that you already are a fairly good reader. *Heroes* is for students who want to read faster and to increase their understanding of what they read. If you complete all twenty-one units—reading the stories and completing the exercises—you will surely improve both your reading rate and your comprehension.

GROUP ONE

At the 1960 Olympic Games, Wilma Rudolph came from far behind in the 400-meter relay to win a Gold Medal and set a new world record. In two other events she tied and beat world records, becoming the first American woman ever to win three Gold Medals in track. She had overcome incredible obstacles of poverty and major physical handicaps to become the world's fastest woman.

Wilma Rudolph: Against the Odds

The moment had come. The runners finished their warm-up exercises. On that August day in 1960, everyone in the Olympic Stadium watched as the fastest women in the world prepared to compete in the 400-meter relay.

When the pistol sounded, the first runners dashed from their starting blocks. There were four women on each team, and each woman had to run one hundred meters—one "leg" of the race. As the first runners completed their leg, each had to pass a baton, or stick, to the next runner on her team. It was the fourth runner for each team who would carry the baton across the finish line.

The Germans got off to a good start, but the Americans were faster. After the first three legs, the Americans led the Germans by about two yards.

The last runner for the United States was a young black woman named Wilma Rudolph. As the third American raced toward her, Wilma readied herself for the pass. The audience watched tensely as the baton was passed to Wilma. Then a gasp went up from the crowd. It was a bad pass. Wilma was forced to stop to pick up the fumbled baton. As she did so, Germany's Jutta Heine went flying by to take the lead.

America's only hope now was that Wilma Rudolph could somehow muster the strength and the speed to catch the fleet German runner. Most people did not know it, but this was not the first time Wilma had faced overwhelming odds.

From the moment she was born in 1940, Wilma Glodean Rudolph had to fight hard. She weighed just four and a half pounds at birth. Her parents feared she would not survive. But she did survive, and slowly her strength grew. After a few weeks, the Rudolphs were able to take her home. There she joined her fifteen brothers and sisters in their rented cottage in Clarksville, Tennessee.

For a while Wilma's health continued to improve. But when she was four years old she was stricken with double pneumonia and scarlet fever. Again her life was in danger, but again Wilma pulled through. That time, however, she was left with a paralyzed left leg.

Doctors in the small town of Clarksville told Mrs. Rudolph that her daughter would never walk again, but Mrs. Rudolph refused to believe it. Instead, she carried her small daughter to the bus terminal and took her on a forty-five-mile bus trip to a clinic in Nashville.

At the clinic, doctors examined Wilma's leg closely. After many tests, they came to a conclusion. They made no promises, but told Mrs. Rudolph that there was one hope. If Wilma could have special heat and water massages at the clinic every day, she might someday be able to walk again.

Mrs. Rudolph could not take Wilma to the clinic every day. The family was poor, the clinic was a long distance away, and there were fifteen other children to care for at home. Besides, Mrs. Rudolph had to work six days a week as a maid to help support the family.

Mrs. Rudolph decided that there was only one thing to do. She must learn to give the special massages to Wilma herself. From the doctors, she learned the special massage technique. For the next two years, Wilma's mother massaged her daughter's leg every day. Usually she sat rubbing the leg until long after little Wilma had fallen asleep. Three of the older Rudolph children also learned to give the massage. Soon Wilma was having four treatments a day. In addition, on the one day each week that Mrs. Rudolph did not have to work, she took Wilma to the Nashville clinic for extra treatment.

For almost two years the massages seemed to do no good. Wilma spent all her time confined to a chair or bed. There was no money in the family to buy a wheelchair. By the time she was six, though, Wilma felt strong enough to try walking. She would hop along for a short distance, and then her weak leg would buckle and she would fall. But she did not give up. Determined to overcome her handicap, she kept trying. Gradually she was able to go farther and farther before collapsing. By the time she was eight years old, Wilma could walk with the help of a leg brace. A special shoe was made to support the weak ankle of her left leg. And so, for the first time, Wilma was able to go to school.

But just barely being able to walk was not enough for Wilma. She kept exercising to increase the strength of her left leg. By the time she was eleven, Wilma could walk without the brace or the special shoe. When she was thirteen, she was chosen for the high school basketball team. And at fifteen, she was averaging 32.1 points per game and was selected for the all-state team.

It was during a basketball game that Wilma was discovered by Ed Temple, track coach for Tennessee State University. He thought he saw in her a great runner.

He was not wrong. With his encouragement, in her senior year of high school Wilma applied to Tennessee State University. She was accepted, and became the first person in her family to attend college.

Once in college, Wilma set her sights on the 1960 Olympics. Early in 1960, however, she went into the hospital. Her tonsils had to be removed. The operation interrupted her training schedule, but that didn't stop Wilma. Three weeks after the operation, she was back out on the track practicing. When it came time for the Americans to go to Rome for the 1960 Olympic Games, Wilma was part of the team.

So, as Wilma ran after Germany's Jutta Heine on that August day during the last leg of the 400-meter relay, she once again found the strength to beat the odds. Quickly she closed the gap between herself and Heine. Then, in the final seconds of the race, Wilma pulled ahead. She led the Americans to a gold medal and a new world record.

Wilma Rudolph won three gold medals during the 1960 Olympics. She won the 100-meter dash by three yards, and tied the world record for that event. She also set a new Olympic record when she won the 200-meter dash. She was the first American woman to win three gold medals in track in one Olympic year. The sickly little girl who spent four years as an invalid and another three years in a leg brace had become the fastest female runner in the world. ■

If you have been timed while reading this selection, enter your reading time below. Then turn to the Words per Minute table on page 154 and look up your reading speed (words per minute). Enter your reading speed on the graph on page 156.

READING TIME: Unit 1
_____ : _____
Minutes   *Seconds*

How well did you read?

- *Answer the four types of questions that follow. The directions for each type of question tell you how to mark your answers.*

- *When you have finished all four exercises, check your work by using the answer key on page 150. For each right answer, put a check mark (✔) on the line beside the box. For each wrong answer, write the correct answer on the line.*

- *For scoring each exercise, follow the directions below the questions.*

A FINDING THE MAIN IDEA

Look at the three statements below. One expresses the main idea of the story you just read. A good main idea statement answers two questions: it tells *who* or *what* is the subject of the story, and it answers the understood question *does what?* or *is what?* Another statement is *too broad*, it is vague and doesn't tell much about the topic of the story. The third statement is *too narrow*, it tells about only one part of the story.

Match the statements with the three answer choices below by writing the letter of each answer in the box in front of the statement it goes with.

M—Main Idea   **B—Too Broad**   **N—Too Narrow**

____ ☐ 1. Though doctors said that Wilma Rudolph would never walk again, through courage and hard work she overcame her handicap.

____ ☐ 2. Wilma Rudolph fought and overcame a serious physical handicap and went on to win three Olympic gold medals and become the world's fastest female runner.

____ ☐ 3. Though she began life as a sickly child, Wilma Rudolph became a great athlete.

____ Score 15 points for a correct *M* answer
____ Score 5 points for each correct *B* or *N* answer
____ TOTAL SCORE: Finding the Main Idea

B RECALLING FACTS

How well do you remember the facts in the story you just read?
Put an *x* in the box in front of the correct answer to each of the
multiple-choice questions below.

1. In the 400-meter relay at the 1960 Olympic Games,
   Wilma Rudolph ran the
   ____ ☐ a. first leg.
   ____ ☐ b. third leg.
   ____ ☐ c. last leg.

2. After the bad baton pass, the German team
   ____ ☐ a. took the lead.
   ____ ☐ b. increased its lead by two yards.
   ____ ☐ c. won the race despite a fast finish by Wilma
             Rudolph.

3. When Wilma Rudolph was born, her parents
   ____ ☐ a. thought she had scarlet fever.
   ____ ☐ b. feared she would not survive.
   ____ ☐ c. knew she would one day be a great athlete.

4. The special treatment that doctors suggested for
   Wilma Rudolph's leg was
   ____ ☐ a. daily massages.
   ____ ☐ b. warm blankets.
   ____ ☐ c. a leg brace.

5. The first sport in which Wilma became involved in
   high school was
   ____ ☐ a. field hockey.
   ____ ☐ b. track.
   ____ ☐ c. basketball.

Score 5 points for each correct answer

____ TOTAL SCORE: Recalling Facts

C MAKING INFERENCES

An inference is a judgment that is made or an idea that is
arrived at based on facts or on information that is given. You
make an inference when you understand something that is *not*
stated directly, but that is *implied* or suggested by the facts that
are given.

Below are five statements that are judgments or ideas that
have been arrived at from the facts of the story. Write the letter
C in the box in front of each statement that is a correct inference. Write the letter F in front of each faulty inference.

C—Correct Inference   F—Faulty Inference

____ ☐ 1. If Wilma Rudolph had been born strong and
          healthy she would not have become a great
          runner.

____ ☐ 2. Part of the credit for Wilma Rudolph's success
          belongs to her mother and her family.

____ ☐ 3. The doctors in the town in which Wilma lived as
          a child were not as knowledgeable about
          medicine as were the doctors at the clinic.

____ ☐ 4. Wilma did not compete in any more races after
          the 1960 Olympics.

____ ☐ 5. Wilma Rudolph was the fastest of the four
          American runners in the 400-meter relay race.

Score 5 points for each correct answer

____ TOTAL SCORE: Making Inferences

D USING WORDS PRECISELY

Each of the numbered sentences below contains an underlined word or phrase from the story you have just read. Under the sentence are three definitions. One has the *same* meaning as the underlined word or phrase, one has *almost the same* meaning, and one has the *opposite* meaning. Match the definitions with the three answer choices by writing the letter that stands for each answer in the box in front of the definition it goes with.

S—Same   A—Almost the Same   O—Opposite

1. The audience watched <u>tensely</u> as the baton was passed to Wilma.

____ ☐ a. nervously

____ ☐ b. anxiously

____ ☐ c. calmly

2. America's only hope now was that Wilma Rudolph could somehow muster the strength and the speed to catch the <u>fleet</u> German runner.

____ ☐ a. sprightly

____ ☐ b. slow

____ ☐ c. swift

3. Wilma spent all her time <u>confined</u> to a chair or bed.

____ ☐ a. free to move

____ ☐ b. bound

____ ☐ c. restricted

4. She would hop along for a short distance, and then her weak leg would <u>buckle</u> and she would fall.

____ ☐ a. give way

____ ☐ b. straighten up

____ ☐ c. weaken

5. The sickly little girl who spent four years as an <u>invalid</u> and another three years in a leg brace had become the fastest female runner in the world.

____ ☐ a. worn-out person

____ ☐ b. disabled person

____ ☐ c. healthy person

____ Score 3 points for each correct *S* answer
____ Score 1 point for each correct *A* or *O* answer

____ TOTAL SCORE: Using Words Precisely

● *Enter the four total scores in the spaces below, and add them together to find your Critical Reading Score. Then record your Critical Reading Score on the graph on page 157.*

_____ Finding the Main Idea
_____ Recalling Facts
_____ Making Inferences
_____ Using Words Precisely

_____ CRITICAL READING SCORE: Unit 1

In the midst of hundreds of men screaming and crying in panic, four people kept their heads. They were the army chaplains on the S.S. Dorchester. The passengers aboard this particular ship were on their way to fight in World War II. Before they reached the battlefields, however, the war stretched out its mighty arm and struck them down. Most of the men died in the cold, dark waters of the North Atlantic that night. But because of the faith and love of the four chaplains, over two hundred lived to tell the story of the Dorchester's last hours.

The Four Chaplains

The men aboard the S.S. *Dorchester* waited in fear. Although the ship's band was playing, the soldiers paid little attention to the music. At 9 P.M. the captain of the ship had announced that the *Dorchester* was being followed by a submarine. The 904 men on board knew that meant trouble. It was February 2, 1943, the middle of World War II. The *Dorchester* was heading toward Greenland with American soldiers and sailors. From Greenland the men would be sent on to Europe to fight in the war. But if a German submarine had seen the ship, the men might never reach land. The Germans could torpedo and sink the *Dorchester* at any moment.

Frightened, the men could think and talk of nothing but the submarine. And the more they talked, the more nervous they got. While most of the people on the ship were scared, however, four men stayed calm. They were the army chaplains assigned to the *Dorchester*. Reverend George Fox and Reverend Clark Poling were Protestant. Father John Washington was Catholic. And Chaplain Alexander Goode was Jewish. Although they represented different religions, the chaplains worked together to soothe the troops.

By midnight the chaplains had quieted many of the men and sent them to their cabins to rest. An hour later, the *Dorchester* was struck by a torpedo. The men burst from their cabins in terror. They raced to the deck to find out what damage had been done. It had been a direct hit. The ship was sinking.

The captain ordered all men to their lifeboat stations. They had to abandon ship. At that command, the men fell apart. The fear that had been lying just below the surface suddenly exploded into panic. Some men jumped overboard without lifejackets. Their bodies quickly grew numb in the frigid water of the North Atlantic. Without lifejackets to keep them afloat, they soon sank to watery graves.

Meanwhile, the men who had stayed on board were scrambling into the wrong lifeboats. Most didn't stop to think that they had been assigned to a particular one. They just headed for the first boat they saw. There were fourteen lifeboats on the *Dorchester*, each designed to hold fifty people. In the confusion, however, one hundred people or more were climbing into a single boat. When the overloaded boats hit the water, the excess weight caused them to sink or overturn. Of the fourteen lifeboats, only two were used correctly.

The chaplains knew they had to do something. They could not simply climb into a lifeboat and float away. They felt it was their duty to stay with the ship. They wanted to do whatever they could to save the troops. So they fought their way through the swarms of terrified men until they reached the box in which the ship's lifejackets were stored. Each grabbed an armful of the jackets and began handing them out.

Many young men were too scared to think clearly. Some didn't want to put on the lifejackets. They just wanted to jump off the sinking ship as quickly as possible. Others were afraid to leave the ship at all. They wanted to hide in their cabins or wait on the deck for someone to rescue them. The chaplains tried desperately to reason with the men. They persuaded many to put on lifejackets before jumping into the open sea. They also coaxed many of the frightened men into lifeboats. When the lifeboats had all been launched, the chaplains continued handing out lifejackets, urging men to jump into the water. They knew that in the water the men would have at least a small chance of survival.

Before long, however, the supply of lifejackets was gone. Without hesitating, the chaplains took off their own and gave them to four soldiers. The four men who were offered those gifts of life didn't want to accept them. But the chaplains insisted. "You must take them," said

Father Washington. "That is an order."

After giving up their one hope of survival, the chaplains turned to comfort the others who were left on the sinking ship. As the bow of the *Dorchester* sank lower and lower, everyone gathered at the ship's stern. There the chaplains linked arms and led the group in singing hymns. As the sea closed in around them, they stopped singing and began to pray aloud. They prayed in English, in Latin and in Hebrew. They were still praying together as the ship took its final plunge and sank to the bottom of the sea.

By the next morning, rescuers had managed to save some of the people in the lifeboats. They had also picked up some men who were floating in the water with lifejackets. In all, 229 men survived to recount the *Dorchester*'s last hours.

When the survivors told of the heroic actions of the four chaplains, people throughout the world honored those brave and selfless men. Three of the four chaplains left wives. Two left small children. The U.S. Army honored the men with Distinguished Service Crosses, which were given to their families. The families took comfort in the knowledge that the chaplains, through their calm work in a crisis, had saved the lives of dozens of young soldiers. And when their work was done and it was time for them to save themselves, they had made the ultimate sacrifice. They had given up their own lifejackets to save the lives of four more people. ■

If you have been timed while reading this selection, enter your reading time below. Then turn to the Words per Minute table on page 154 and look up your reading speed (words per minute). Enter your reading speed on the graph on page 156.

READING TIME: Unit 2
_____ : _____
Minutes   *Seconds*

How well did you read?

- *Answer the four types of questions that follow. The directions for each type of question tell you how to mark your answers.*

- *When you have finished all four exercises, check your work by using the answer key on page 150. For each right answer, put a check mark (✓) on the line beside the box. For each wrong answer, write the correct answer on the line.*

- *For scoring each exercise, follow the directions below the questions.*

A FINDING THE MAIN IDEA

Look at the three statements below. One expresses the main idea of the story you just read. A good main idea statement answers two questions: it tells *who* or *what* is the subject of the story, and it answers the understood question *does what?* or *is what?* Another statement is *too broad,* it is vague and doesn't tell much about the topic of the story. The third statement is *too narrow,* it tells about only one part of the story.

Match the statements with the three answer choices below by writing the letter of each answer in the box in front of the statement it goes with.

M—Main Idea   **B—Too Broad**   **N—Too Narrow**

____ ☐ 1. After the torpedo hit the *S.S. Dorchester,* many of the men panicked and jumped overboard or ran to the wrong lifeboats.

____ ☐ 2. The four chaplains saved dozens of men and even sacrificed their own lives so others could live.

____ ☐ 3. The chaplains aboard the *S.S. Dorchester* showed great courage in the face of disaster.

____ Score 15 points for a correct *M* answer
____ Score 5 points for each correct *B* or *N* answer
____ TOTAL SCORE: Finding the Main Idea

B RECALLING FACTS

How well do you remember the facts in the story you just read? Put an x in the box in front of the correct answer to each of the multiple-choice questions below.

1. The S.S. *Dorchester* was headed toward
   - ____ ☐ a. Iceland.
   - ____ ☐ b. Germany.
   - ____ ☐ c. Greenland.

2. At 9 P.M. on February 2, 1943, the captain told the troops
   - ____ ☐ a. that they were being followed by a submarine.
   - ____ ☐ b. to abandon ship.
   - ____ ☐ c. to go to their lifeboat stations.

3. Each lifeboat on the *Dorchester* was designed to hold
   - ____ ☐ a. one hundred people.
   - ____ ☐ b. fifty people.
   - ____ ☐ c. twenty-five people.

4. When the box of lifejackets was empty, the chaplains
   - ____ ☐ a. looked for another box of lifejackets.
   - ____ ☐ b. gave away their own lifejackets to four other men.
   - ____ ☐ c. encouraged the men to jump into the water without lifejackets.

5. As the stern of the ship finally plunged into the icy water, the four chaplains were
   - ____ ☐ a. singing together.
   - ____ ☐ b. praying aloud.
   - ____ ☐ c. comforting others on the ship.

Score 5 points for each correct answer

____ TOTAL SCORE: Recalling Facts

C MAKING INFERENCES

An inference is a judgment that is made or an idea that is arrived at based on facts or on information that is given. You make an inference when you understand something that is *not* stated directly, but that is *implied*, or suggested by the facts that are given.

Below are five statements that are judgments or ideas that have been arrived at from the facts of the story. Write the letter *C* in the box in front of each statement that is a correct inference. Write the letter *F* in front of each faulty inference.

C—Correct Inference   F—Faulty Inference

- ____ ☐ 1. The S.S. *Dorchester* was the first ship torpedoed by the Germans in World War II.

- ____ ☐ 2. If all fourteen lifeboats had been properly used, more men would have survived.

- ____ ☐ 3. The four chaplains all held the same religious beliefs.

- ____ ☐ 4. One of the duties of chaplains is to stay calm during times of great danger.

- ____ ☐ 5. The chaplains knew that if they gave up their own lifejackets they would almost certainly die.

Score 5 points for each correct answer

____ TOTAL SCORE: Making Inferences

D USING WORDS PRECISELY

Each of the numbered sentences below contains an underlined word or phrase from the story you have just read. Under the sentence are three definitions. One has the *same* meaning as the underlined word or phrase, one has *almost the same* meaning, and one has the *opposite* meaning. Match the definitions with the three answer choices by writing the letter that stands for each answer in the box in front of the definition it goes with.

S—Same   A—Almost the Same   O—Opposite

1. When the overloaded lifeboats hit the water, the <u>excess</u> weight caused them to sink or overturn.

____ ☐ a. extra

____ ☐ b. insufficient

____ ☐ c. great

2. So they fought their way through the <u>swarms</u> of terrified men until they reached the box in which the ship's lifejackets were stored.

____ ☐ a. groups

____ ☐ b. small clusters

____ ☐ c. active crowds

3. Their bodies quickly grew numb in the <u>frigid</u> water of the North Atlantic.

____ ☐ a. chilly

____ ☐ b. freezing

____ ☐ c. hot

4. When the survivors told of the heroic actions of the four chaplains, people throughout the world honored those brave and <u>selfless</u> men.

____ ☐ a. self-centered

____ ☐ b. kind

____ ☐ c. unselfish

5. And when their work was done and it was time for them to save themselves, they had made the <u>ultimate</u> sacrifice.

____ ☐ a. greatest possible

____ ☐ b. lowest

____ ☐ c. important

____ Score 3 points for each correct S answer

____ Score 1 point for each correct A or O answer

____ TOTAL SCORE: Using Words Precisely

● *Enter the four total scores in the spaces below, and add them together to find your Critical Reading Score. Then record your Critical Reading Score on the graph on page 157.*

_____ Finding the Main Idea
_____ Recalling Facts
_____ Making Inferences
_____ Using Words Precisely
_____ CRITICAL READING SCORE: Unit 2

When professional baseball first began in the United States, it was a white man's sport—no colored people allowed. Blacks who wanted to play the game had to play in the black leagues. The prejudice was strong, so when Jackie Robinson joined the Brooklyn Dodgers as the first black player in the major leagues, he had a tough battle on his hands. And the only way to win it was by not fighting. That called for the greatest strength of all.

Jackie Robinson: The Loneliest Season

The meeting lasted three hours. Branch Rickey, general manager of the Brooklyn Dodgers, didn't want to take any chances. He wanted to make sure he had the right man for the job. The right man had to be willing to endure great public abuse. He had to be willing to "turn the other cheek." It was no task for a coward or a hothead. Rickey was looking for a black man to break into the whites-only world of major league baseball.

At that meeting on August 28, 1945, the baseball player being interviewed was Jackie Robinson. Jackie listened as Rickey explained why he wanted a black man on his team. Rickey was tired of seeing black talent go to waste. He knew that a man with Jackie's athletic ability could help the Dodgers. Jackie's superb talents might even lead the Dodgers to a pennant.

But being the first black man in the major leagues would not be easy. Rickey warned Jackie that there would be trouble. He gave Jackie a taste of the kind of name-calling that he would have to face. If Jackie couldn't take such insults from one man, what chance would he have against a crowd of forty thousand hostile fans? And it wouldn't be just the fans who would be hostile. Rickey pointed out that many of the white players would resent having a black man in the league.

It would be a dangerous situation. Jackie's presence could result in all kinds of violence. It could even lead to riots. Rickey knew that there was only one way it could work. If Jackie took the job, he would have to promise to avoid doing anything that would aggravate the already tense situation. He would have to remain silent in the face of vicious racial slurs and threats of violence. After telling Jackie all those things, Rickey paused and asked, "Well? Do you still want to go through with it?" Without hesitation, Jackie answered, "Yes. I am not afraid to try."

Who was this courageous man named Jackie Robinson? He was a man with great physical power, speed and coordination. He was also a man of great moral character. The youngest of five children, Jackie was born in Cairo, Georgia, in 1919. Shortly after Jackie's birth, his father deserted the family. Jackie's mother moved her family to California in the hope that there would be more job opportunities there. She found work as a maid and fought hard to keep her family together. She did all she could to give her children a sense of self-worth and pride.

Despite his mother's support, life was not easy for Jackie. For a young black boy in the 1930s, California was not much better than rural Georgia. White children often called him "nigger." Many restaurants, playgrounds and movie theaters were closed to him. Even the Pasadena municipal swimming pool was "for whites only."

Somehow Jackie survived the discrimination of those years without losing his dreams. He hoped to go to college and to become a baseball player. Jackie did manage to get into a junior college, and from there he made it to the University of Southern California at Los Angeles (UCLA). At UCLA he ran track and joined the basketball and football teams. But baseball remained his real love.

When World War II broke out, Jackie joined the army and became a second lieutenant. Racial hatred followed him into the service. One day a bus driver ordered Jackie to move to the back of an army bus. The front, he said, was reserved for whites. Jackie became angry and refused to move. His refusal led to his arrest and trial in a military court. Although he was found innocent, he never forgot the insult. He told himself that he never wanted to be insulted like that again.

Then in August of 1945, he found himself sitting in Branch Rickey's office promising to endure even worse insults in silence. Jackie knew it would be difficult for him to control his temper. But like Rickey, Jackie knew that it was the only way he could ever play major-league ball. So he decided to try.

After one highly successful year on the Dodgers' Triple-A farm team, Jackie was ready for the big time. So in the spring of 1947 Jackie Robinson put on a Dodger uniform for the first time. He was finally in the big leagues—big league baseball and big league racism. When the other members of the team heard of Jackie's arrival, several of them threatened to quit. Rickey talked to them, however, and got them to agree to try one season with Jackie in their midst. But they warned that if at the end of that time they were still unhappy they would either quit or asked to be traded to another team.

When the official season opened in April, Jackie was a starting player for the Dodgers. But he had to play a position he had never played before. Jackie was an experienced second baseman. Unfortunately, the Dodgers already had a good man in that position. So Jackie was forced to play first base. When he took to the field on opening day, his mind was on how he would handle his new assignment. But his thoughts were soon interrupted by the booing and hissing of the crowd. He heard the fans jeering at him and calling him names. But just as he had promised

Rickey, he did not react. He ignored the fans completely.

Gradually Jackie got used to the rude gestures and angry cries of the white fans. At every game, he had to put up with abuse from the stands. On top of that, he usually had to endure the hatred of the opposing team. When Jackie stepped up to bat, many pitchers threw the baseball directly at his head. When he was in the field, runners would try to step on his shoe, jabbing their spikes into his foot. Even Jackie's own teammates offered him little support.

As the season wore on, Jackie grew discouraged. It seemed he was making no progress. The fans continued to taunt him without mercy, and the players still did not accept him. Jackie began to wonder if it was worth all the pain and humiliation he was suffering. But something inside him would not let him give up. He continued to play and to endure. One sportswriter writing during that long summer of 1947 referred to Jackie as "the loneliest man I have ever seen in sports."

But lonely or not, Jackie Robinson's patience and persistence finally paid off. By the end of the season, he was triumphant. He batted .297, led the league in stolen bases, and was named Rookie of the Year. His daring baserunning and strong hitting also helped the Dodgers win their first pennant in six years.

Jackie's superior athletic skill earned him the respect of his teammates and fellow athletes. By September, only one Dodger still wanted to be traded to another team, and most of the sports fans in America were on Jackie's side.

Jackie Robinson played ten years in the major leagues and was elected to the National Baseball Hall of Fame after his retirement. Most importantly, he opened the door for other great black athletes. Baseball was eventually blessed by such legends as Willie Mays, Hank Aaron and Reggie Jackson. While the talents of those men were tremendous, it was Jackie Robinson's willingness to suffer hatred and humiliation that made their careers possible. ■

If you have been timed while reading this selection, enter your reading time below. Then turn to the Words per Minute table on page 154 and look up your reading speed (words per minute). Enter your reading speed on the graph on page 156.

READING TIME: Unit 3
_____ : _____
Minutes   *Seconds*

How well did you read?

- *Answer the four types of questions that follow. The directions for each type of question tell you how to mark your answers.*

- *When you have finished all four exercises, check your work by using the answer key on page 150. For each right answer, put a check mark (✔) on the line beside the box. For each wrong answer, write the correct answer on the line.*

- *For scoring each exercise, follow the directions below the questions.*

A FINDING THE MAIN IDEA

Look at the three statements below. One expresses the main idea of the story you just read. A good main idea statement answers two questions: it tells *who* or *what* is the subject of the story, and it answers the understood question *does what?* or *is what?* Another statement is *too broad*, it is vague and doesn't tell much about the topic of the story. The third statement is *too narrow*, it tells about only one part of the story.

Match the statements with the three answer choices below by writing the letter of each answer in the box in front of the statement it goes with.

M—Main Idea   **B—Too Broad**   **N—Too Narrow**

_____ ☐ 1. Jackie Robinson, a gifted black athlete, led the Brooklyn Dodgers to the pennant in 1947.

_____ ☐ 2. Jackie Robinson was a great baseball player who was discriminated against because he was black.

_____ ☐ 3. Jackie Robinson endured great personal abuse to become the first black baseball player in the major leagues.

_____ Score 15 points for a correct *M* answer
_____ Score 5 points for each correct *B* or *N* answer
_____ TOTAL SCORE: Finding the Main Idea

B RECALLING FACTS

How well do you remember the facts in the story you just read?
Put an *x* in the box in front of the correct answer to each of the
multiple-choice questions below.

1. One of the reasons Branch Rickey asked Jackie
   Robinson to play for the Brooklyn Dodgers was
   that he
   - ☐ a. wanted to win the pennant.
   - ☐ b. thought Jackie would attract big crowds.
   - ☐ c. could pay Jackie less than other players.

2. Shortly after Jackie was born, his father
   - ☐ a. moved to California.
   - ☐ b. deserted the family.
   - ☐ c. died suddenly.

3. When Jackie Robinson joined the Dodgers in 1947,
   - ☐ a. some players threatened to quit.
   - ☐ b. Branch Rickey was fired.
   - ☐ c. he had just gotten out of the army.

4. During his first year with the Dodgers, Jackie
   Robinson played
   - ☐ a. first base.
   - ☐ b. second base.
   - ☐ c. third base.

5. Jackie Robinson played in the major leagues for
   - ☐ a. one year.
   - ☐ b. ten years.
   - ☐ c. five years.

Score 5 points for each correct answer

_____ TOTAL SCORE: Recalling Facts

C MAKING INFERENCES

An inference is a judgment that is made or an idea that is
arrived at based on facts or on information that is given. You
make an inference when you understand something that is *not*
stated directly, but that is *implied*, or suggested by the facts that
are given.

Below are five statements that are judgments or ideas that
have been arrived at from the facts of the story. Write the letter
C in the box in front of each statement that is a correct inference. Write the letter *F* in front of each faulty inference.

C—Correct Inference   F—Faulty Inference

1. Branch Rickey thought that black athletes were
   much better than white athletes.

2. If Jackie Robinson had not been a top quality
   player on a top team, he would probably not
   have been accepted in the end.

3. During the 1930s and 1940s, discrimination
   against black Americans existed only in the
   southern United States.

4. Jackie Robinson had no hope that racial
   discrimination in the United States would
   someday disappear.

5. The black baseball players who followed
   Robinson into the majors did not have as
   difficult a time as he did.

Score 5 points for each correct answer

_____ TOTAL SCORE: Making Inferences

D USING WORDS PRECISELY

Each of the numbered sentences below contains an underlined word or phrase from the story you have just read. Under the sentence are three definitions. One has the *same* meaning as the underlined word or phrase, one has *almost the same* meaning, and one has the *opposite* meaning. Match the definitions with the three answer choices by writing the letter that stands for each answer in the box in front of the definition it goes with.

S—Same   A—Almost the Same   O—Opposite

1. The right man had to be willing to endure great public <u>abuse</u>.

 ____ ☐ a. mistreatment

 ____ ☐ b. acceptance

 ____ ☐ c. violence

2. Rickey pointed out that many of the white players would <u>resent</u> having a black man in the league.

 ____ ☐ a. dislike

 ____ ☐ b. feel angry about

 ____ ☐ c. welcome

3. If Jackie took the job, he would have to promise to avoid doing anything that would <u>aggravate</u> the already tense situation.

 ____ ☐ a. make worse

 ____ ☐ b. upset

 ____ ☐ c. improve

4. He would have to remain silent in the face of vicious racial <u>slurs</u> and threats of violence.

 ____ ☐ a. insults

 ____ ☐ b. compliments

 ____ ☐ c. impolite remarks

5. The fans continued to <u>taunt</u> him without mercy, and the players still did not accept him.

 ____ ☐ a. encourage

 ____ ☐ b. tease

 ____ ☐ c. jeer at

____ Score 3 points for each correct *S* answer
____ Score 1 point for each correct *A* or *O* answer

____ TOTAL SCORE: Using Words Precisely

● *Enter the four total scores in the spaces below, and add them together to find your Critical Reading Score. Then record your Critical Reading Score on the graph on page 157.*

_____ Finding the Main Idea
_____ Recalling Facts
_____ Making Inferences
_____ Using Words Precisely

_____ CRITICAL READING SCORE: Unit 3

Cesar Chavez: Uniting Farm Workers

Cesar Chavez spent his entire childhood in poverty. He was born in 1927 in Arizona, where he lived until he was eleven years old. His parents, who were both Mexican, struggled to eke out a living by raising chickens, watermelons and vegetables on their farm. Then in 1938, the Chavez family went broke. To survive, Cesar and his family became migrant workers, traveling from place to place, following the California crops. If there were walnuts to pick in southern California, that was where they went. When cherries were ready for harvesting in the north, they moved north. Although they worked hard, they did not earn much money. Growers refused to pay migrant workers fair wages. If a worker complained about the pay, the grower simply fired him or her. By 1939 there were three hundred thousand migrant workers in California, so growers could always find another person to do the job.

It didn't take Cesar Chavez long to discover how dismal the life of a migrant worker was. He spent countless days sweating in the hot California sun as he stooped to pick peas for less than a penny a pound. He dug so many beets out of the wet Sacramento soil that the skin on his fingers cracked open. At night he and his family stayed in wretched cabins at the labor camps. They often had to share a bathroom with as many as fifty other families. One winter, when they had no money for rent, they were forced to live in a cold, wet tent.

Whenever Cesar wasn't working, he went to school. But even that was an unpleasant experience. The other children laughed at his Mexican accent. They made fun of him because he didn't have any shoes. They called him names and constantly threatened to beat him up. Because his family moved so often, he never stayed in one school long enough to make many friends. Between the ages of eleven and fifteen, he attended more than thirty different schools.

When Cesar was twenty-one years old, he married a woman named Helen. Four years later he got his first steady job. He became a staff member of the Community Service Organization, a group dedicated to protecting the civil rights of Mexican-Americans. The group fought discrimination by encouraging Mexican-Americans to register to vote.

Cesar worked for that organization until 1962. By then he and Helen had eight children. The family was not rich, but they had enough money to pay the bills. They also had a few hundred dollars in the bank.

Still, Cesar was not satisfied. He knew that the majority of Mexican-Americans were not as lucky as he was. Most were still migrant farm workers with little hope for regular jobs or permanent homes. Cesar wanted desperately to help those farm workers. He felt that there was only one way they could improve their situation. All the workers had to join together. They had to form a union.

Cesar believed that he could organize such a union. But he knew it would not be easy. He would have to quit his job. His savings would soon be used up, and then he would be facing a return to the kind of poverty he had known as a child. He spent many nights talking it over with Helen. Finally, with her support, he took the big step. He resigned from his job and set out to organize a farm workers' union.

His plan was to win over the workers one at a time. To do that, he had to talk to them in person. For the next few weeks he traveled all over California. In just three months he covered almost fifteen thousand miles. He went out into the fields picking peas and staking grapes with workers, just to get a chance to talk to them. He invited many of them to his home to share his family's meager meals.

Each time he met with a worker, he explained that the union would fight for

fair wages. It would demand better working conditions. It would do everything possible to protect the rights of farm workers. Cesar also told the workers that the union would never use violence to win its battles. He knew that in order to be successful the union would need public support. Because the public did not approve of violence, Cesar Chavez planned to use negotiations, strikes and boycotts to fight the growers.

As word of Cesar's work spread, his dream of uniting farm workers became known as *La Causa*. That is a Spanish phrase that means "the cause." Before long, Cesar found other Mexican-Americans who were willing to work for *La Causa* without pay. Just as the movement began to gain momentum, however, Cesar ran out of money. Unwilling to give up, he began to work part-time picking grapes. Helen also went to work as a farm laborer. The Chavez family scrimped on food, heat and winter clothing in order to continue their work with *La Causa*.

On September 30, 1962, Cesar and his fellow workers officially founded the union. In 1965 the union, which became known as the United Farm Workers Association, still had just a few thousand members. Nonetheless, in the fall of that

If you had managed to climb out of severe poverty, would you willingly put yourself back into it? As a child, Cesar Chavez went without shoes and often without a home, and he had to do the work of a man, under terrible conditions. Yet, after he had earned a good job and a house, he decided to give them up. He risked his own comfort for a cause—to help poor working people gain dignity and respect; to teach them to work together to get what was rightfully theirs.

year Cesar took on a powerful enemy. For the next five years he and the union were locked in a battle with the grape growers of California.

The struggle began when the Filipino grape pickers decided to go on strike. The pickers were angry because the growers of table grapes had just lowered wages by more than 25 percent. The members of the United Farm Workers Association took a vote and decided to join the Filipinos. All the grape pickers in the union went on strike.

The growers were outraged, and tried every way they could to break the strike. They sent guards out to harass the strikers. They beat striking workers and threatened to have Cesar Chavez killed. They even sprayed picket lines with pesticides.

But the workers believed strongly in what they were doing, and they did not give up. As Cesar had hoped, the public became upset by the violent tactics of the growers. Public opinion turned away from them. More and more people began to support the striking laborers. Cesar was pleased to see that, but he wanted to gain even more public support. So late in 1967, he decided to start a boycott of California grapes. He would ask the public to stop buying California grapes, as a show of support for the workers. He hoped the boycott would last until the growers agreed to negotiate with the union.

To start the boycott, Cesar sent fifty workers to New York City. The workers picketed stores where California grapes were sold. New Yorkers responded by supporting the boycott. The picketers then went to other cities and did the same thing. They found the people in those cities willing to help them too.

Although the boycott was successful, the grape growers still refused to accept the union. At that point, some union members grew impatient. They had been without work for over two years. They had families to support. They were desperate for food and money. In their frustration, they began to talk of violence. The only way to get the grape companies to listen, they said, was to kill a few growers.

Cesar tried to stop that kind of talk, but the workers wouldn't listen. Cesar worried that La Causa was losing sight of its goals. He felt that he had to find a way to make the union members stop and think. He decided to go on a fast. When the union members heard about it, they began visiting him to talk about the situation. As the farm workers rallied around him, they were reminded of the principles of La Causa. Soon all talk of violence ceased. Cesar himself grew weaker and weaker. The lack of food permanently damaged his health. But the fast worked. The spirit of the union members grew stronger. Finally, after twenty-five days, Cesar began to eat again. When he did, the union members were more determined and more united than ever before.

The struggle against the grape growers did not end here. It took two more years of strikes and boycotts before any real progress was made. But in 1970, the California grape growers gave in. They signed the first union contracts with farm workers. It had been a long and bitter battle. Ninety-five percent of the striking workers had been forced to sell their homes and their cars just to survive. And there were still many more battles to be fought. There were no union contracts yet for workers who picked lettuce, celery, broccoli or strawberries.

Cesar Chavez knew all that, and he was determined to continue the battle. He decided to keep fighting until all crop growers treated their workers with fairness and respect. As he led his union into those new battles, he became a symbol for all oppressed workers. La Causa continued to gain support. And Cesar Chavez continued to stress the importance of unity and nonviolence in the struggle for justice. ∎

If you have been timed while reading this selection, enter your reading time below. Then turn to the Words per Minute table on page 154 and look up your reading speed (words per minute). Enter your reading speed on the graph on page 156.

READING TIME: Unit 4

_____ : _____
Minutes   Seconds

How well did you read?

- *Answer the four types of questions that follow. The directions for each type of question tell you how to mark your answers.*

- *When you have finished all four exercises, check your work by using the answer key on page 150. For each right answer, put a check mark (✔) on the line beside the box. For each wrong answer, write the correct answer on the line.*

- *For scoring each exercise, follow the directions below the questions.*

A FINDING THE MAIN IDEA

Look at the three statements below. One expresses the main idea of the story you just read. A good main idea statement answers two questions: it tells *who* or *what* is the subject of the story, and it answers the understood question *does what?* or *is what?* Another statement is *too broad*, it is vague and doesn't tell much about the topic of the story. The third statement is *too narrow*, it tells about only one part of the story.

Match the statements with the three answer choices below by writing the letter of each answer in the box in front of the statement it goes with.

M—Main Idea   B—Too Broad   N—Too Narrow

_____ ☐ 1. Cesar Chavez worked for many years and made great personal sacrifices to form a union to protect the rights of farm workers.

_____ ☐ 2. Cesar Chavez was a Mexican-American who cared a great deal about migrant farm workers.

_____ ☐ 3. Cesar Chavez helped win rights for California grape pickers by organizing a long and successful boycott of California table grapes.

_____ Score 15 points for a correct *M* answer

_____ Score 5 points for each correct *B* or *N* answer

_____ TOTAL SCORE: Finding the Main Idea

B RECALLING FACTS

How well do you remember the facts in the story you just read? Put an x in the box in front of the correct answer to each of the multiple-choice questions below.

1. When Cesar Chavez quit his job, he
   - ____ ☐ a. was living in a tent.
   - ____ ☐ b. had a few thousand dollars in the bank.
   - ____ ☐ c. was the father of eight children.

2. Because his family moved so often, Cesar
   - ____ ☐ a. never went to school.
   - ____ ☐ b. dropped out of school when he was eleven years old.
   - ____ ☐ c. went to more than thirty different schools.

3. In an effort to break the grape pickers' strike, grape growers
   - ____ ☐ a. brought in Filipino workers.
   - ____ ☐ b. sprayed striking workers with pesticides.
   - ____ ☐ c. raised wages 25 percent.

4. When union members heard of Cesar's fast, they
   - ____ ☐ a. began to fast too.
   - ____ ☐ b. went to visit him.
   - ____ ☐ c. threatened to use violence to get him to eat again.

5. By the end of the strike against the grape growers,
   - ____ ☐ a. several grape growers had been killed.
   - ____ ☐ b. Cesar was ready to give up his leadership of the union.
   - ____ ☐ c. most strikers had lost their homes.

Score 5 points for each correct answer

____ TOTAL SCORE: Recalling Facts

C MAKING INFERENCES

An inference is a judgment that is made or an idea that is arrived at based on facts or on information that is given. You make an inference when you understand something that is *not* stated directly, but that is *implied*, or suggested by the facts that are given.

Below are five statements that are judgments or ideas that have been arrived at from the facts of the story. Write the letter C in the box in front of each statement that is a correct inference. Write the letter F in front of each faulty inference.

C—Correct Inference   F—Faulty Inference

- ____ ☐ 1. Cesar Chavez loved being a migrant worker.
- ____ ☐ 2. Cesar Chavez didn't care if his children grew up in poverty.
- ____ ☐ 3. Before the boycott, many Americans were not aware of the working conditions of migrant farm laborers.
- ____ ☐ 4. If Cesar Chavez had not fasted, the farm workers would have begun to use violence.
- ____ ☐ 5. The only crop that Filipinos picked was grapes.

Score 5 points for each correct answer

____ TOTAL SCORE: Making Inferences

D USING WORDS PRECISELY

Each of the numbered sentences below contains an underlined word or phrase from the story you have just read. Under the sentence are three definitions. One has the *same* meaning as the underlined word or phrase, one has *almost the same* meaning, and one has the *opposite* meaning. Match the definitions with the three answer choices by writing the letter that stands for each answer in the box in front of the definition it goes with.

S—Same   A—Almost the Same   O—Opposite

1. He became a staff member of the Community Service Organization, a group <u>dedicated</u> to protecting the civil rights of Mexican-Americans.

   ____ ☐ a. uncertain

   ____ ☐ b. willing

   ____ ☐ c. committed

2. At night he and his family stayed in <u>wretched</u> cabins at the labor camps.

   ____ ☐ a. miserable

   ____ ☐ b. unpleasant

   ____ ☐ c. delightful

3. As word of Cesar's work spread, his dream of <u>uniting</u> farm workers became known as *La Causa*.

   ____ ☐ a. dividing

   ____ ☐ b. gathering

   ____ ☐ c. bringing together

4. They sent guards out to <u>harass</u> the strikers.

   ____ ☐ a. annoy slightly

   ____ ☐ b. help greatly

   ____ ☐ c. bother repeatedly

5. As the farm workers rallied around him, they were reminded of the <u>principles</u> of *La Causa*.

   ____ ☐ a. ideas

   ____ ☐ b. reasons against

   ____ ☐ c. guiding beliefs

____ Score 3 points for each correct *S* answer

____ Score 1 point for each correct *A* or *O* answer

____ TOTAL SCORE: Using Words Precisely

● *Enter the four total scores in the spaces below, and add them together to find your Critical Reading Score. Then record your Critical Reading Score on the graph on page 157.*

_____	Finding the Main Idea
_____	Recalling Facts
_____	Making Inferences
_____	Using Words Precisely
_____	CRITICAL READING SCORE: Unit 4

It seemed that all his dreams would have to end. What good is an athlete with one leg? Friends and relatives thought that he would have to sit out life on the sidelines. But Terry Fox knew differently. He wasn't about to give up being who he was. With one strong leg and one made of steel and fiberglass, he determined to run across a continent. Terry Fox proved that with hope, courage, and belief in yourself, you can achieve incredible things.

Terry Fox and the Marathon of Hope

Terry Fox was just eighteen years old when he learned that he had bone cancer. It was a terrible shock. He had always been so healthy and athletic. In high school he had been named athlete of the year. As a student at Simon Fraser University in Vancouver, Canada, he was playing soccer and basketball. He was even dreaming of a career in professional sports. But when the doctors found cancer in his leg, those dreams were shattered.

The discovery of Terry's cancer came as a shock. One morning Terry woke up with a sharp pain in his right leg. As the day went on, the pain grew worse. Frightened, he checked himself into a local hospital to try to find out what was wrong. The doctors found cancer in the bone of Terry's right knee. They had to move quickly. Two days later they operated to amputate Terry's right leg above the knee.

The amputation did not end the problem. Terry still had to undergo eighteen months of painful chemotherapy —treatment with drugs—to prevent the spread of the cancer. He was fitted with an artificial leg made of steel and fiberglass. He had to learn how to walk on the new leg. And he had to adjust to being a sports spectator instead of a player.

It was the last adjustment that was hardest for Terry. He was not ready to give up his dream of being a professional athlete. While recovering from his operation, he began playing basketball in a wheelchair, and he continued to think about the sports he loved. Every day he saw the tired faces of the other patients in the cancer ward. Many of them had given up hope. But Terry refused to give up. He refused to stop dreaming.

One day in the winter of 1978, he read a magazine article about a one-legged runner. The story inspired Terry. He decided that he too could become a one-legged runner. He would prove to people that cancer victims could still be athletes. They might lose their arms or legs, but they did not have to lose their courage or their willingness to fight. He decided to run all the way across Canada. He would do it dressed in jogging shorts so people could see that he had an artificial leg. It would be a run to raise money for cancer research. And it would be a run to prove to himself and to the world that he was still a fighter.

At first no one took Terry seriously. Even his mother thought he was crazy. How could anyone with an artificial leg limp across a continent? And Terry wasn't talking about going in a straight line from coast to coast. He was planning a 5,300-mile route that would take him through the most populated areas. But Terry was determined to do it. He got the backing of the Canadian Cancer Society. Then he organized a fund-raising dance and sought the support of businesses.

He began his training by hobbling a half mile. The next day he ran twice that far. Over the next fourteen months he ran longer and longer distances. He had no coach. He had nobody cheering him on. But he kept training because he did not want to be a quitter. He wanted to make his dream come true. As people in his home town watched him hopping down the road every day, they began to believe in him. Finally, by April of 1980, he had put in over three thousand miles of training. He could run twenty-five to thirty miles a day. He was ready to begin his impossible journey.

On the morning of April 12, 1980, Terry Fox stood on the shore of the Atlantic Ocean, on the coast of Newfound-land. He wore a T-shirt that bore the words "Marathon of Hope." As a few close friends and family members watched, he dipped his artificial leg into the cold water. He vowed to start running and to keep running until he dipped his leg into the Pacific Ocean on the other side of Canada.

Terry hoped to average twenty-five miles a day. He slept in the homes of friends or with people who volunteered to put him up for the night. Each morning he got up at four o'clock to eat, and was ready to go by 5 A.M. Along the way he faced many obstacles. Twice he was nearly run off the road by trucks. The police barred him from running on the Trans-Canadian Highway because he was a traffic hazard. He endured snow, rain and hailstones the size of golf balls. Worst of all, his artificial leg kept getting loose. Once a welder had to do spot repairs on the metal limb. Despite all the difficulties, Terry often ran as much as thirty miles a day.

Soon the Canadian people began to take notice of Terry's gallant run. They winced at the sight of the one-legged youth hobbling mile after mile on endless highways. As they heard the story behind his run, they rushed to send money to the Canadian Cancer Society. Within a month Terry had raised a hundred thousand dollars for cancer research. It seemed that his efforts just might bring in the one million dollars he was aiming for. Well-wishers began to gather along his route. Hockey stars Bobby Orr and Darryl Sittler met him along the way to cheer him on. The Prime Minister of Canada, Pierre Trudeau, also went out to encourage Terry. Every day, radio and television programs played a song called "Run, Terry, Run."

By mid-July Terry had traveled over two thousand miles. He had reached Toronto.

There he was greeted by ten thousand fans. People wept to see him struggling down the road in his awkward, hopping run. They clapped, shouted and cheered as he ran by. Even police officers were moved to tears by his bravery and determination.

But Terry was not to reach the Pacific Ocean. A few weeks after leaving Toronto he knew something was wrong. He began coughing. A sharp pain kept flashing through his neck and chest. For three days he tried to ignore it. He knew he should probably stop running and see a doctor. But he still did not want to give up.

On the fourth day after the pain had begun, he was up early and running hard as usual. He was in northern Ontario, nearing a city called Thunder Bay. After running eighteen miles, he began to have trouble breathing.

Suddenly he started to choke. The pain in his chest was almost unbearable. But by that time he was in the middle of the city. Crowds had gathered along the sides of the road. He later said, "There was no way I was going to stop running then, not with all those people there."

So he struggled on. He had to run another mile before he was out of the city and away from the crowds. Then, when there were no more people in sight, Terry Fox stopped. He had run 3,336 miles and had raised over two million dollars.

Terry was rushed to the hospital for tests. The doctors examined him while an anxious Canada waited for the news. Then it came. He met with reporters and said

simply, "I've got it in my lungs." The cancer that had taken his right leg had spread. His journey had ended.

On June 28, 1981, Terry Fox died. A few days before his death, a postage stamp was dedicated in his honor. It was the first time in Canadian history that such an honor was given to a living person. He was also awarded the Order of Canada, the highest civilian medal. His funeral was carried on national radio and television. Flags across Canada were flown at half-mast. The Canadian people then donated an incredible twenty-five million dollars to cancer research in his name.

Terry Fox's impossible run touched the lives of many people. His strength and optimism gave new hope to cancer victims and other handicapped people. As Prime Minister Trudeau put it, "Terry Fox's courage and awesome determination inspired this country as no one else has ever done." ■

If you have been timed while reading this selection, enter your reading time below. Then turn to the Words per Minute table on page 154 and look up your reading speed (words per minute). Enter your reading speed on the graph on page 156.

READING TIME: Unit 5

———— : ————
Minutes   *Seconds*

How well did you read?

- *Answer the four types of questions that follow. The directions for each type of question tell you how to mark your answers.*

- *When you have finished all four exercises, check your work by using the answer key on page 150. For each right answer, put a check mark (✔) on the line beside the box. For each wrong answer, write the correct answer on the line.*

- *For scoring each exercise, follow the directions below the questions.*

A   FINDING THE MAIN IDEA

Look at the three statements below. One expresses the main idea of the story you just read. A good main idea statement answers two questions: it tells *who* or *what* is the subject of the story, and it answers the understood question *does what?* or *is what?* Another statement is *too broad*, it is vague and doesn't tell much about the topic of the story. The third statement is *too narrow*, it tells about only one part of the story.

Match the statements with the three answer choices below by writing the letter of each answer in the box in front of the statement it goes with.

M—Main Idea   B—Too Broad   N—Too Narrow

____ ☐ 1. Running across Canada with one artificial leg, Terry Fox inspired a nation and raised millions of dollars for cancer research.

____ ☐ 2. Terry Fox was a courageous young man who inspired an entire nation.

____ ☐ 3. Terry Fox fought to become an athlete, even though he lost one leg to cancer.

____ Score 15 points for a correct *M* answer
____ Score 5 points for each correct *B* or *N* answer

____ TOTAL SCORE: Finding the Main Idea

B RECALLING FACTS

How well do you remember the facts in the story you just read? Put an x in the box in front of the correct answer to each of the multiple-choice questions below.

1. Terry Fox started his run at
   - ☐ a. the shore of the Atlantic Ocean.
   - ☐ b. the shore of the Pacific Ocean.
   - ☐ c. Thunder Bay, Ontario.

2. Terry Fox had dreamed of a career in
   - ☐ a. cancer research.
   - ☐ b. fund-raising.
   - ☐ c. sports.

3. Terry began his training by
   - ☐ a. getting up at 4 A.M.
   - ☐ b. finding a coach to help him.
   - ☐ c. hobbling a half mile.

4. Terry Fox was forced to stop his "Marathon of Hope" because the cancer had spread to his
   - ☐ a. neck.
   - ☐ b. lungs.
   - ☐ c. back.

5. Terry Fox was the first person to
   - ☐ a. be awarded the Order of Canada.
   - ☐ b. have his funeral carried on national radio and television.
   - ☐ c. have a postage stamp dedicated to him while he was still alive.

Score 5 points for each correct answer

_____ TOTAL SCORE: Recalling Facts

C MAKING INFERENCES

An inference is a judgment that is made or an idea that is arrived at based on facts or on information that is given. You make an inference when you understand something that is *not* stated directly, but that is *implied*, or suggested by the facts that are given.

Below are five statements that are judgments or ideas that have been arrived at from the facts of the story. Write the letter C in the box in front of each statement that is a correct inference. Write the letter F in front of each faulty inference.

C—Correct Inference   F—Faulty Inference

1. If the doctors had not amputated Terry Fox's leg, he would have died earlier.

2. Terry Fox would not have been as admired if he had lived to make it to the Pacific Ocean.

3. Many people contributed to the Canadian Cancer Society for the first time because of Terry Fox.

4. The cancer would not have spread to Terry's lungs if he had not pushed himself so hard physically.

5. If the cancer had not spread to Terry Fox's lungs, he would have one day dipped his leg into the Pacific Ocean.

Score 5 points for each correct answer

_____ TOTAL SCORE: Making Inferences

D USING WORDS PRECISELY

Each of the numbered sentences below contains an underlined word or phrase from the story you have just read. Under the sentence are three definitions. One has the *same* meaning as the underlined word or phrase, one has *almost the same* meaning, and one has the *opposite* meaning. Match the definitions with the three answer choices by writing the letter that stands for each answer in the box in front of the definition it goes with.

S—Same   A—Almost the Same   O—Opposite

1. Along the way he faced many <u>obstacles</u>.

____ ☐ a. difficulties

____ ☐ b. frustrations

____ ☐ c. easy stretches

2. The police <u>barred</u> him from running on the Trans-Canadian Highway because he was a traffic hazard.

____ ☐ a. helped

____ ☐ b. prohibited

____ ☐ c. outlawed

3. He <u>endured</u> snow, rain and hailstones the size of golf balls.

____ ☐ a. stood up under

____ ☐ b. conquered

____ ☐ c. met with

4. Soon the Canadian people began to take notice of Terry's <u>gallant</u> run.

____ ☐ a. cowardly

____ ☐ b. courageous

____ ☐ c. daring

5. They <u>winced</u> at the sight of the one-legged youth hobbling mile after mile on endless highways.

____ ☐ a. stared boldly

____ ☐ b. frowned

____ ☐ c. flinched

____ Score 3 points for each correct *S* answer
____ Score 1 point for each correct *A* or *O* answer

____ TOTAL SCORE: Using Words Precisely

● *Enter the four total scores in the spaces below, and add them together to find your Critical Reading Score. Then record your Critical Reading Score on the graph on page 157.*

_____ Finding the Main Idea
_____ Recalling Facts
_____ Making Inferences
_____ Using Words Precisely

_____ CRITICAL READING SCORE: Unit 5

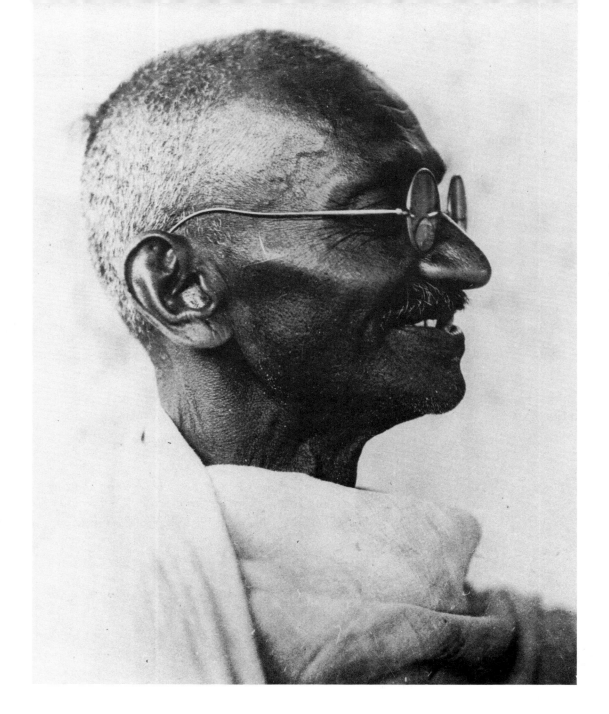

Though he was totally against violence, Mahatma Gandhi led the people of India in their successful struggle for independence from Britain. The struggle, however, was a peaceful one. Gandhi taught his followers to simply act according to what they believed was right, and to resist living in ways that they believed to be wrong. One of the strongest acts of nonviolent resistance that Gandhi led was a march to the sea to collect salt. This simple act required great courage, for it directly challenged the right of Britain to rule India.

Mahatma Gandhi: The Peaceful Way

To most people, salt is just something to sprinkle on popcorn. But to the people of India, salt is something special. It is a symbol of their struggle for independence from Britain. It is a symbol of the Salt March of 1930, which was a turning point in that struggle. And it is a symbol of Mahatma Gandhi, the man who led the Salt March.

Gandhi believed that India should be a free country. He did not like seeing his people ruled by foreigners. The Salt March was his way of protesting one aspect of British rule. The British had passed a law making it illegal for the people of India to collect their own salt. Everyone was required to buy salt from the British. In early 1930, Gandhi believed it was time to break that law. He decided to walk to the sea to gather his own salt "from the ocean created by God."

It was not the first time that Gandhi had decided to break the law. He had been leading protests against British rule for years. Many of the protests had been illegal, and Gandhi had often been jailed. But he didn't mind. He believed that if a law was morally wrong it was his duty to break it. That was part of his philosophy, which he called Satyagraha (suh-TYAH-gruh-huh). The philosophy called for the use of moral force to change the wrongs of society. A person who used Satyagraha did not hate his enemies. He did not ever use violence against them. But neither did he give in. According to Satyagraha, a person should act in a way that was morally right, and sooner or later the forces of right would win out. A person practicing Satyagraha would not follow ways that he or she believed to be wrong.

In March of 1930, Gandhi wrote to the British viceroy, or governor, stating his intention to lead a salt march. The viceroy did not reply. So on March 12, Gandhi and seventy-five followers set out on the march. Gandhi was sixty-one years old.

On the march, Gandhi wore only a simple loincloth. In his right hand he carried a thick bamboo staff to lean on as he walked. Day after day, the hot sun beat down on him and his followers. Still they kept walking, averaging ten miles a day. As they walked, they were joined by hundreds of other Indians. Every step of the way, people poured out of their huts to greet Gandhi and join in the march. The revered leader stopped frequently to speak to the people. He reminded them of their duty to love one another and to resist the British through nonviolent means. Gandhi told his followers, "I would rather die a dog's death and have my bones licked by dogs than that I should return home a broken man."

Throughout the march, Gandhi watched for the arrival of the viceroy's soldiers. He fully expected to be arrested. He had even named a substitute to take over leadership of the march after his arrest. But days passed and no soldiers showed up. The viceroy had decided not to make an arrest, because he thought the march would simply peter out and die. He was wrong.

The Salt March soon became world news. People from many different countries followed Gandhi's every move. They marveled at the thin old man who was capturing the love and admiration of the Indian people. Every day, Gandhi was offered a ride in a cart. But he always refused. He insisted on walking all the way. He knew the world was watching and waiting.

Finally, on April 5, Gandhi reached the coast. By that time almost ten thousand people were marching with him. Gandhi was feeling weak. He had walked 241 miles. The trip had tired him. But he was also very happy, and when a reporter asked him what he wanted from the march, he said, "I want world sympathy in this battle of Right against Might."

All that night Gandhi and his followers prayed by the water's edge. Early the next morning, Gandhi held a religious ceremony and bathed briefly in the sea to purify himself. Then, at 8:30 A.M., he stooped by the water's edge to pick up a handful of salt. Thousands of Indians shouted their joy. For the first time in their lives, all the people who had marched with Gandhi felt truly free.

After picking up the salt, Gandhi was sure he would be arrested immediately. But he was not. It was another three weeks before the British put him in jail. In the meantime, the news of his defiance spread all across India. The word *salt* was on everyone's lips. Almost overnight, it came to mean independence for India. The people were in an uproar. Many of them followed Gandhi's example by going down to the sea and gathering salt for themselves. They also began burning British cloth in the streets and holding public demonstrations against Britain.

On April 27, Gandhi was finally arrested for his role in the Salt March. As he was taken to jail, he calmly began singing his favorite hymn. He was not upset or worried. His faith in Satyagraha remained unshaken. He was certain that sooner or later Britain would have to give up its unjust position as ruler of India.

In the end, Britain did grant India the right of self-government. But that did not happen quickly. India's fight for independence had only begun with the Salt March. It took another seventeen years for the country to win its freedom. During those seventeen years, Gandhi was arrested again and again. Some of his followers were beaten and even killed. But Gandhi never abandoned his belief in nonviolent protest. And with Gandhi as their leader, neither did the people of India. ∎

If you have been timed while reading this selection, enter your reading time below. Then turn to the Words per Minute table on page 154 and look up your reading speed (words per minute). Enter your reading speed on the graph on page 156.

READING TIME: Unit 6
_____ : _____
Minutes *Seconds*

How well did you read?

- *Answer the four types of questions that follow. The directions for each type of question tell you how to mark your answers.*

- *When you have finished all four exercises, check your work by using the answer key on page 150. For each right answer, put a check mark (✔) on the line beside the box. For each wrong answer, write the correct answer on the line.*

- *For scoring each exercise, follow the directions below the questions.*

A FINDING THE MAIN IDEA

Look at the three statements below. One expresses the main idea of the story you just read. A good main idea statement answers two questions: it tells *who* or *what* is the subject of the story, and it answers the understood question *does what?* or *is what?* Another statement is *too broad*, it is vague and doesn't tell much about the topic of the story. The third statement is *too narrow*, it tells about only one part of the story.

Match the statements with the three answer choices below by writing the letter of each answer in the box in front of the statement it goes with.

M—Main Idea   **B—Too Broad**   **N—Too Narrow**

_____ ☐ 1. Mahatma Gandhi was a much-loved and respected moral leader of the Indian people.

_____ ☐ 2. Gandhi led the people of India in a nonviolent struggle for independence, beginning with a march to the sea to collect salt, in defiance of British law.

_____ ☐ 3. In 1930, Mahatma Gandhi led thousands of Indian people on an illegal march to the sea to collect salt.

_____ Score 15 points for a correct *M* answer
_____ Score 5 points for each correct *B* or *N* answer

_____ TOTAL SCORE: Finding the Main Idea

B RECALLING FACTS

How well do you remember the facts in the story you just read? Put an *x* in the box in front of the correct answer to each of the multiple-choice questions below.

1. Under British rule it was illegal for Indians to
   - ___ ☐ a. gather salt.
   - ___ ☐ b. buy salt.
   - ___ ☐ c. use salt.

2. A person living according to the philosophy of Satyagraha uses
   - ___ ☐ a. physical force.
   - ___ ☐ b. illegal force.
   - ___ ☐ c. moral force.

3. Immediately after receiving Gandhi's letter in March of 1930, the viceroy
   - ___ ☐ a. called out his troops.
   - ___ ☐ b. put Gandhi in jail.
   - ___ ☐ c. did nothing.

4. The first thing Gandhi did when he reached the coast was
   - ___ ☐ a. pray with his followers.
   - ___ ☐ b. pick up a handful of salt.
   - ___ ☐ c. bathe briefly in the sea to purify himself.

5. Three weeks after the Salt March,
   - ___ ☐ a. India was granted independence.
   - ___ ☐ b. Gandhi was arrested.
   - ___ ☐ c. the people of India revolted against the British.

Score 5 points for each correct answer

___ TOTAL SCORE: Recalling Facts

C MAKING INFERENCES

An inference is a judgment that is made or an idea that is arrived at based on facts or on information that is given. You make an inference when you understand something that is *not* stated directly, but that is *implied*, or suggested by the facts that are given.

Below are five statements that are judgments or ideas that have been arrived at from the facts of the story. Write the letter *C* in the box in front of each statement that is a correct inference. Write the letter *F* in front of each faulty inference.

C—Correct Inference   F—Faulty Inference

- ___ ☐ 1. The British did not view Satyagraha the way that Gandhi did.
- ___ ☐ 2. The people of India needed salt more than the people of other countries did.
- ___ ☐ 3. Gandhi felt it was important to the cause that he personally walk all the way to the sea.
- ___ ☐ 4. Gandhi was pleased when the reports of his Salt March appeared in newspapers around the world.
- ___ ☐ 5. The salt law was not the only British law that upset Gandhi and the Indian people.

Score 5 points for each correct answer

___ TOTAL SCORE: Making Inferences

D USING WORDS PRECISELY

Each of the numbered sentences below contains an underlined word or phrase from the story you have just read. Under the sentence are three definitions. One has the *same* meaning as the underlined word or phrase, one has *almost the same* meaning, and one has the *opposite* meaning. Match the definitions with the three answer choices by writing the letter that stands for each answer in the box in front of the definition it goes with.

S—Same   A—Almost the Same   O—Opposite

1. The viceroy had decided not to make an arrest, because he thought the march would simply peter out.

____ ☐ a. gather strength

____ ☐ b. slowly die out

____ ☐ c. slow down

2. They marveled at the thin old man who was capturing the love and admiration of the Indian people.

____ ☐ a. were filled with wonder by

____ ☐ b. were not interested in

____ ☐ c. were surprised by

3. But he was also very happy, and when a reporter asked him what he wanted from the march, he said, "I want world sympathy in this battle of Right against Might."

____ ☐ a. understanding

____ ☐ b. opposition

____ ☐ c. support

4. In the meantime, the news of his defiance spread all across India.

____ ☐ a. open rebellion

____ ☐ b. obedience

____ ☐ c. misbehavior

5. His faith in Satyagraha remained unshaken.

____ ☐ a. weak

____ ☐ b. in place

____ ☐ c. firm

____ Score 3 points for each correct *S* answer
____ Score 1 point for each correct *A* or *O* answer

____ TOTAL SCORE: Using Words Precisely

● *Enter the four total scores in the spaces below, and add them together to find your Critical Reading Score. Then record your Critical Reading Score on the graph on page 157.*

_____ Finding the Main Idea
_____ Recalling Facts
_____ Making Inferences
_____ Using Words Precisely

_____ **CRITICAL READING SCORE: Unit 6**

Against incredible odds, Gladys Aylward set out to lead a hundred small children across the mountains of war-torn China to a place of safety. She had little hope of succeeding, but she never considered escaping alone. Her children needed her, and she did not let them down.

Gladys Aylward: Journey to Safety

The sun was just rising as Gladys Aylward prepared to set out across the wild and rugged mountains of China. She had to hurry. The Japanese soldiers were just a few hours from her village. Gladys was sorry to be leaving. For ten years she had worked as a missionary in the remote hills of northern China. The people there had grown to like and trust her. But now, in 1940, China was at war with Japan. The Japanese were invading through northern China, and they were killing everyone they met along the way. Most Chinese civilians had already left the area.

As Gladys packed her few belongings, she tried not to think about the bullet wound in her back. Only twenty-four hours earlier, a Japanese soldier had spotted her in a field and had fired at her. One of his bullets had grazed her back. Although the wound was not serious, it caused her great pain.

She also tried not to think about how tired and hungry she was. Instead, she turned her attention to the children who were sleeping in every corner of the house. There were a hundred of them, all orphans. After their parents had been killed in the war, they had gone to Gladys for shelter. Most of them were very young—between four and eight years old. Only a handful were over ten. Gladys could not leave the children to be killed by the Japanese. She planned to take them all with her.

That would not be an easy thing to do. In fact, it would be almost impossible. They would have to walk over steep, rocky mountains that offered few trails. None of the children had good shoes. The small children could not walk far in a day. Even if they did get over the mountains, they would still have to cross the Yellow River, which was more than a mile wide. Only then could they get a train to Sian, a city where they would be safe.

Gladys knew that the journey would take several weeks. They would have to cover over 250 difficult miles. She also knew that her food supply would not last more than three or four days. By herself, she could probably make it. But how far would she get with a hundred children? It didn't matter. Not for a moment did she consider leaving the children behind. She had to try to get them all safely to Sian. She had to try.

She quickly woke the children and helped them collect their belongings. Every child carried his or her own blanket, bowl and chopsticks. The small children were excited. To them it was a great adventure. As the group began walking, the little ones scrambled ahead over the rocks, laughing and shouting.

By noontime, however, they were hungry. They stopped by a mountain stream, and Gladys boiled some water in the iron pot she had brought along. Lunch was nothing more than boiled dough strings, but the children didn't mind. They had been eating the mushy strands of dough all their lives. They ate so much, in fact, that Gladys got only a couple of spoonfuls. She did not complain, though, and from then on, two or three spoonfuls was her usual ration.

After lunch the children perked up. They walked several more miles before it got dark. As night fell, they came to the edge of a small village. Gladys found an old temple where the children could sleep. They were all so tired that they slept soundly. They did not notice the rats that swarmed over their bodies in the night.

The next few nights, the travelers were not lucky enough to find any villages. They had to sleep out among the rocks, with only their thin blankets to keep them warm. As the group struggled on, the children's spirits began to droop. By then the children had holes in their shoes, and the bottoms of their feet were cut, blistered and bleeding. They had used up their entire supply of food and were growing steadily weaker.

Gladys began carrying the blankets of the weakest ones. She also let the little ones take turns riding on her shoulders. Each day the scorching rays of the sun beat down on them. They had no water, and they passed no rivers or streams. The children's skin became burned, and their lips cracked. On top of all that, they ran out of trails to follow. They had to scramble over huge boulders and down jagged cliffs.

Gladys tried hard to keep up the children's hopes. As they marched bravely along, she taught them hymns and told them stories. But by the seventh day she was worried. They had been without food for three days. She feared that if they did not find a village soon they would all die. Suddenly one of the older boys began shouting. "Soldiers!" he screamed. "Soldiers are coming!" Gladys felt panic rise within her. If the soldiers were Japanese, they would surely kill her and the children.

Luckily, the soldiers were Chinese. When Gladys told them of her plight, they reached into their knapsacks and pulled out enough food to feed Gladys and all the hungry children.

After the soldiers left, Gladys and the children moved on. For the next four days, they stumbled through the mountains. Many of the children were so tired and hungry that they cried constantly. Others had such sore feet that they could hobble only a hundred yards before stopping to rest. Gladys was getting weaker too, but

she kept singing and talking and urging them on. She knew that their only hope was to keep going.

At last they reached a mountain peak from which they could see the Yellow River below. The children cheered as they hurried down toward the distant river. Along the way they came to a deserted village. Gladys sent the children out to scour the town for food. They found only some moldy grain, a few old dough cakes and some vegetable scraps. Still, it was better than nothing. When they reached the river, Gladys threw all the food into her pot and boiled it up. Then she gave it to the children. Although she ate nothing, each child got a whole bowl full of food.

At that point the travelers faced a new problem. How were they going to get across the river? It was much too wide and deep to ford or swim, and there were no boats in the area. For the next three days they waited, helpless, by the water. Gladys prayed that a boat would pass by. On the third day, help finally arrived. A Chinese soldier found them and arranged to have a boat carry them all across the river. On the other side of the river was a village where the half-starved children were given a good meal. Then they boarded a train headed for Sian.

Their adventures, however, were not quite over. Part of the train tracks had been destroyed. So once again Gladys had to take the children into the mountains.

Finally, they reached Sian. By that time Gladys was so weak that she could barely

think straight. Still, she managed to get the children to an orphanage. There they received food, clothing and shelter. She had done it. By some miracle of determination and luck, she had led a hundred children safely across the mountains of China.

Shortly after the journey ended, Gladys Aylward collapsed and was taken to a hospital. Doctors discovered that she had been suffering from typhus for weeks. She had a temperature of 105 degrees and was developing pneumonia. For months the doctors didn't know if she would live. Eventually, though, she recovered and continued her missionary work. Although she later returned to her native England, Gladys Aylward never forgot the children she had saved during the war. And they never forgot her. They thought of her always as their mother. ■

If you have been timed while reading this selection, enter your reading time below. Then turn to the Words per Minute table on page 154 and look up your reading speed (words per minute). Enter your reading speed on the graph on page 156.

READING TIME: Unit 7

_____ : _____
Minutes   *Seconds*

How well did you read?

- *Answer the four types of questions that follow. The directions for each type of question tell you how to mark your answers.*

- *When you have finished all four exercises, check your work by using the answer key on page 150. For each right answer, put a check mark (✔) on the line beside the box. For each wrong answer, write the correct answer on the line.*

- *For scoring each exercise, follow the directions below the questions.*

A FINDING THE MAIN IDEA

Look at the three statements below. One expresses the main idea of the story you just read. A good main idea statement answers two questions: it tells *who* or *what* is the subject of the story, and it answers the understood question *does what?* or *is what?* Another statement is *too broad,* it is vague and doesn't tell much about the topic of the story. The third statement is *too narrow,* it tells about only one part of the story.

Match the statements with the three answer choices below by writing the letter of each answer in the box in front of the statement it goes with.

M—Main Idea   B—Too Broad   N—Too Narrow

_____ ☐ 1. Gladys Aylward rescued a hundred homeless Chinese children by leading them on a difficult journey across the mountains of China.

_____ ☐ 2. Gladys Aylward was a missionary who spent many years helping the people of China.

_____ ☐ 3. Gladys kept the children's spirits up enough for them to keep walking, even when they were starving and in pain.

_____ Score 15 points for a correct *M* answer

_____ Score 5 points for each correct *B* or *N* answer

_____ TOTAL SCORE: Finding the Main Idea

B RECALLING FACTS

How well do you remember the facts in the story you just read? Put an *x* in the box in front of the correct answer to each of the multiple-choice questions below.

1. Most of the children who struggled over the mountains were between
   - ___ ☐ a. three and six years old.
   - ___ ☐ b. four and eight years old.
   - ___ ☐ c. ten and twelve years old.

2. On the first night of the journey, Gladys and the children slept
   - ___ ☐ a. out in the open among the rocks.
   - ___ ☐ b. in an old temple.
   - ___ ☐ c. in a deserted village.

3. Gladys tried to keep the children's spirits up by
   - ___ ☐ a. singing songs and telling stories.
   - ___ ☐ b. carrying the children's blankets, bowls and chopsticks for them.
   - ___ ☐ c. stopping to let the children swim in mountain streams.

4. One of the biggest problems Gladys and the children faced was
   - ___ ☐ a. blinding snowstorms.
   - ___ ☐ b. wild animals.
   - ___ ☐ c. lack of food.

5. Upon reaching Sian, Gladys took the children to
   - ___ ☐ a. their parents.
   - ___ ☐ b. a temple.
   - ___ ☐ c. an orphanage.

Score 5 points for each correct answer

___ TOTAL SCORE: Recalling Facts

C MAKING INFERENCES

An inference is a judgment that is made or an idea that is arrived at based on facts or on information that is given. You make an inference when you understand something that is *not* stated directly, but that is *implied,* or suggested by the facts that are given.

Below are five statements that are judgments or ideas that have been arrived at from the facts of the story. Write the letter *C* in the box in front of each statement that is a correct inference. Write the letter *F* in front of each faulty inference.

C—Correct Inference   F—Faulty Inference

- ___ ☐ 1. Women and children were often killed in the war between China and Japan.
- ___ ☐ 2. If the Japanese had not been invading northern China, Gladys would have stayed in her village.
- ___ ☐ 3. Gladys Aylward's first concern was for her own safety.
- ___ ☐ 4. All civilians leaving northern China during that time followed the same route that Gladys followed.
- ___ ☐ 5. Gladys finally returned to England because she was driven out of China.

Score 5 points for each correct answer

___ TOTAL SCORE: Making Inferences

58

D USING WORDS PRECISELY

Each of the numbered sentences below contains an underlined word or phrase from the story you have just read. Under the sentence are three definitions. One has the *same* meaning as the underlined word or phrase, one has *almost the same* meaning, and one has the *opposite* meaning. Match the definitions with the three answer choices by writing the letter that stands for each answer in the box in front of the definition it goes with.

S—Same   A—Almost the Same   O—Opposite

1. For ten years she had worked as a missionary in the <u>remote</u> hills of northern China.

____ ☐ a. located far from places having many people

____ ☐ b. close to large, highly-populated cities

____ ☐ c. wild and unsettled

2. One of his bullets had <u>grazed</u> her back.

____ ☐ a. scraped

____ ☐ b. cut across the surface

____ ☐ c. traveled clean through

3. When Gladys told them of her <u>plight</u>, they reached into their knapsacks and pulled out enough food to feed Gladys and all the hungry children.

____ ☐ a. bad situation

____ ☐ b. uncomfortable situation

____ ☐ c. good fortune

4. Others had such sore feet that they could <u>hobble</u> only a few hundred yards before stopping to rest.

____ ☐ a. walk slowly

____ ☐ b. walk freely

____ ☐ c. limp painfully

5. Gladys sent the children out to <u>scour</u> the town for food.

____ ☐ a. look quickly about

____ ☐ b. hunt around

____ ☐ c. search thoroughly

____ Score 3 points for each correct *S* answer

____ Score 1 point for each correct *A* or *O* answer

____ TOTAL SCORE: Using Words Precisely

● *Enter the four total scores in the spaces below, and add them together to find your Critical Reading Score. Then record your Critical Reading Score on the graph on page 157.*

_____ Finding the Main Idea
_____ Recalling Facts
_____ Making Inferences
_____ Using Words Precisely

_____ CRITICAL READING SCORE: Unit 7

GROUP TWO

For Matthew Henson there was no fame, no place in the history books. When the news went out to the world that the North Pole had finally been conquered, his name was not mentioned. Yet without him, the renowned explorer Robert Peary would not have succeeded in becoming the first man to reach the top of the world. It was Henson's strength and determination that pushed the expedition through its final, agonizing steps.

Matthew Henson: To the Top of the World

It took Commander Robert E. Peary eighteen years and nine separate attempts to reach the North Pole. Each attempt required a superhuman effort. No one had ever reached the North Pole. Many men had tried, but all had failed. Some had even lost their lives trying to cross the difficult terrain from Greenland to the very top of the world. On each expedition, Peary faced starvation, blinding sun and endless Arctic winters. Most people today think of Commander Peary as a hero. Indeed, his actions did show tremendous bravery. But what most people don't know is that there is a second hero in this story. He accompanied Peary on every journey to the North. He saved Peary's life on several occasions, and made his ultimate success possible. The man's name was Matthew Henson.

Matt Henson was a black man born in Charles County, Maryland, in 1867. By the time he was twelve years old, both his parents had died and he had gone to work as a cabin boy on a merchant ship. He never had a chance to go to school, but the captain of the ship taught him to read and write. When the captain died in 1884, Henson became a stockboy in a hat store. He longed for adventure, but as a black man in a prejudiced white society, there was little chance that he would ever have the opportunity to join in any great undertaking.

In 1887, however, Henson had the good fortune of meeting a man named Robert Peary. Peary was looking for a servant to accompany him on an exploration of Nicaragua. Henson leaped at the chance to go along. Peary and Henson worked well together. In the jungles of Central America they became less like master and servant and more like comrades.

On returning to the United States, Peary announced his plan to try to conquer the North Pole. He could not make the journey alone, of course, but although he was impressed with Henson's work, he didn't think Henson would want to head out to the frigid North. "After all," Peary said, "you are a black man. You work well in warm, sunny climates. But you would find it very difficult to be up north."

Peary probably did not mean this as an insult. He was merely reflecting the ignorance of the times. But to Matthew Henson, the words were a direct challenge. His response was, "I'll go north with you, sir, and I think I'll stand it as well as any man."

Henson's words turned out to be an understatement. To survive in the bitter and barren land of northern Greenland, it was necessary to adopt the lifestyle of the Eskimos. From the beginning, it was Henson who showed the most promise of learning Eskimo ways. This was partly because the Eskimos helped him more than they helped Peary. They spent countless hours teaching him their language and customs. They helped him because they trusted him. Although he was a foreigner, he had dark skin like theirs, so they assumed he was an Eskimo from a foreign land. Also, they liked his kindness, cheerfulness and willingness to learn. Soon the Eskimos not only trusted Henson but loved him, as well.

From the Eskimos, Henson learned to make clothing from animal skins and to build and repair sleds using local tools. Most importantly, he mastered the use of the Eskimo dogsled. Driving a dogsled involved managing a group of ten or more half-wild dogs. The driver had to be able to crack a twenty-eight-foot whip in the air just inches above a dog's head. Henson mastered that difficult skill in just one month.

On their first trip to the Arctic, in 1891, Peary, Henson and the other members of the expedition discovered why no earlier explorers had ever reached the North Pole. The Pole was hundreds of miles beyond the northernmost Eskimo settlement in Greenland. To get past that settlement, Peary's group had to travel in the winter, when the ice around the Pole was thick enough to support the weight of men and dogs. But the winter weather in that part of the world was almost beyond human endurance. The temperature often fell to fifty or sixty degrees below zero. The wind whipped across the ice with bone-chilling fury. Violent snowstorms arose without warning. Some sled dogs became sick and died; others went mad and had to be shot. The game animals that lived in the region began migrating southward, so the group faced the possibility of starvation. And throughout the winter, the men were plagued by frostbite.

Given such bleak conditions, it is not surprising that the expedition did not reach the Pole. In fact, on that trip Peary only got to within five hundred miles of the North Pole. For the next seventeen years, however, he kept trying. Each time, he faced the same dangers. And each time, he had to recruit a new crew. Few people cared to spend more than one winter in the frozen Arctic wasteland of northern Greenland. Only Matt Henson stuck with Peary on every trip for the entire eighteen years.

With every journey to the North, Peary became more and more dependent on Henson. Henson even saved Peary's life several times. On one such occasion, the two men went out on the ice alone to scout a new area. While crossing an ice bridge between two cliffs, Peary stepped on a weak spot. The ice gave way and he fell through up to his armpits. He hung trapped with only his head and shoulders still visible. If he made one false move, he would fall to his death hundreds of feet below. It was Henson's calm response that saved him. Henson quickly grabbed a rope, dropped to his stomach, and crawled out onto the thin ice. As Peary clung to the ice around him, Henson managed to tie a rope around his chest. Then, for fifteen tense minutes, Henson inched his way back, pulling Peary out of the hole to safety.

On another occasion, Henson saved Peary from a charging musk-ox. Peary had fallen to his knees and was watching helplessly as the ox ran toward him. The beast was only a few feet from Peary when Henson grabbed his gun and fired off a shot, killing the ox. On still another trip, Peary developed a severe case of frostbite in his toes. Henson tried to warm the toes by holding them against his own stomach, but that didn't help. Henson then carried Peary back to their ship. The ship's doctor had to cut the toes off to keep gangrene from setting in.

In 1909, on their ninth and final journey to the North, Peary and Henson finally reached their goal. With four Eskimos and about forty dogs, they made it all the way to the North Pole. By that time, Peary was exhausted. Years of struggling against the Arctic climate had weakened him. Henson was tired too, but he had reserves of energy that astonished even Peary.

After taking some photographs and resting for a few hours, the men began the long journey home. Peary lasted only an hour before collapsing. Tears streamed down his face. Like Henson, he had permanent burns and blisters on his eyes from the intense glare of the Arctic sun. But he seemed to have suddenly become almost totally blind. He looked and acted like a tired old man. In a role that had become familiar, Matt Henson rescued Peary. He loaded him onto a sled and, in just sixteen days, dragged him the four hundred miles back to their camp.

In finally reaching the North Pole, Robert Peary became a famous man. He was made an admiral in the Navy, and he retired to a life of ease. For Matt Henson, however, there was no fame, no public recognition. Because he was a black man, no one was interested in his story. Matthew Henson lived the rest of his life in a small apartment in Harlem, a black community in New York City. For a while he worked as a handyman in a garage. Later he became a messenger in the United States Customs House. ∎

If you have been timed while reading this selection, enter your reading time below. Then turn to the Words per Minute table on page 155 and look up your reading speed (words per minute). Enter your reading speed on the graph on page 156.

READING TIME: Unit 8

_____ : _____
Minutes   Seconds

How well did you read?

- *Answer the four types of questions that follow. The directions for each type of question tell you how to mark your answers.*

- *When you have finished all four exercises, check your work by using the answer key on page 151. For each right answer, put a check mark (✓) on the line beside the box. For each wrong answer, write the correct answer on the line.*

- *For scoring each exercise, follow the directions below the questions.*

A FINDING THE MAIN IDEA

Look at the three statements below. One expresses the main idea of the story you just read. A good main idea statement answers two questions: it tells *who* or *what* is the subject of the story, and it answers the understood question *does what?* or *is what?* Another statement is *too broad,* it is vague and doesn't tell much about the topic of the story. The third statement is *too narrow,* it tells about only one part of the story.

   Match the statements with the three answer choices below by writing the letter of each answer in the box in front of the statement it goes with.

M—Main Idea   B—Too Broad   N—Too Narrow

_____ ☐ 1. Matthew Henson, a courageous and loyal black man, made it possible for Robert Peary to be credited as the first man to reach the North Pole.

_____ ☐ 2. Matthew Henson saved Robert Peary's life a number of times on various expeditions to the North Pole.

_____ ☐ 3. Matthew Henson was a brave black man who got no recognition for his part in Robert Peary's expeditions to the North Pole.

_____ Score 15 points for a correct *M* answer

_____ Score 5 points for each correct *B* or *N* answer

_____ TOTAL SCORE: Finding the Main Idea

B RECALLING FACTS

How well do you remember the facts in the story you just read? Put an x in the box in front of the correct answer to each of the multiple-choice questions below.

1. The first place Peary and Henson went together was
   ____ ☐ a. Africa.
   ____ ☐ b. Greenland.
   ____ ☐ c. Nicaragua.

2. When Peary met him, Matthew Henson was working as a
   ____ ☐ a. cabin boy.
   ____ ☐ b. stock boy.
   ____ ☐ c. servant.

3. One of the reasons the Eskimos liked Henson was that he was
   ____ ☐ a. a foreigner.
   ____ ☐ b. dark skinned.
   ____ ☐ c. an Eskimo.

4. Peary and Henson finally reached the North Pole on their
   ____ ☐ a. fifth attempt.
   ____ ☐ b. seventh attempt.
   ____ ☐ c. ninth attempt.

5. The Navy honored Peary by
   ____ ☐ a. making him an admiral.
   ____ ☐ b. giving him a medal.
   ____ ☐ c. retiring him.

Score 5 points for each correct answer

____ TOTAL SCORE: Recalling Facts

C MAKING INFERENCES

An inference is a judgment that is made or an idea that is arrived at based on facts or on information that is given. You make an inference when you understand something that is *not* stated directly, but that is *implied*, or suggested by the facts that are given.

Below are five statements that are judgments or ideas that have been arrived at from the facts of the story. Write the letter *C* in the box in front of each statement that is a correct inference. Write the letter *F* in front of each faulty inference.

C—Correct Inference   F—Faulty Inference

____ ☐ 1. It was not possible to reach the North Pole during the summer months.

____ ☐ 2. The Eskimos knew more about how to survive in the Arctic than anyone else did.

____ ☐ 3. No matter how well the men dressed, when they were in the far North they were always in danger of getting frostbite.

____ ☐ 4. After the first expedition to the North Pole, Henson continued to accompany Peary only out of loyalty to him.

____ ☐ 5. Matthew Henson was honored when he was given the job as a messenger in the United States Customs House.

Score 5 points for each correct answer

____ TOTAL SCORE: Making Inferences

D USING WORDS PRECISELY

Each of the numbered sentences below contains an underlined word or phrase from the story you have just read. Under the sentence are three definitions. One has the *same* meaning as the underlined word or phrase, one has *almost the same* meaning, and one has the *opposite* meaning. Match the definitions with the three answer choices by writing the letter that stands for each answer in the box in front of the definition it goes with.

S—Same   A—Almost the Same   O—Opposite

1. He longed for adventure, but as a black man in a prejudiced white society, there was little chance that he would ever have the opportunity to join in any great undertaking.

   ☐ a. treating certain people unfairly on the basis of an unfounded negative opinion

   ☐ b. choosing to give some people better treatment than others

   ☐ c. fair minded in making judgments

2. In the jungles of Central America they became less like master and servant and more like comrades.

   ☐ a. enemies

   ☐ b. close companions

   ☐ c. partners

3. He was merely reflecting the ignorance of the times.

   ☐ a. lack of understanding

   ☐ b. knowledge

   ☐ c. lack of knowledge

4. To survive in the bitter and barren land of northern Greenland, it was necessary to adopt the lifestyle of the Eskimos.

   ☐ a. choose

   ☐ b. take on

   ☐ c. give up

5. Henson was tired too, but he had reserves of energy that astonished even Peary.

   ☐ a. surprised

   ☐ b. amazed

   ☐ c. did not impress

   ___ Score 3 points for each correct S answer
   ___ Score 1 point for each correct A or O answer
   ___ TOTAL SCORE: Using Words Precisely

- *Enter the four total scores in the spaces below, and add them together to find your Critical Reading Score. Then record your Critical Reading Score on the graph on page 157.*

_____

_____ Finding the Main Idea
_____ Recalling Facts
_____ Making Inferences
_____ Using Words Precisely

_____ CRITICAL READING SCORE: Unit 8

Raoul Wallenberg: Cheating the Death Machine

The women stood clustered together in a street not far from the Danube River in Budapest, Hungary. Many were crying; all were terrified. They were being taken to the Danube by Hungarian soldiers who supported Nazi Germany. The soldiers planned to shoot the women and throw their bodies into the river. The women had committed no crime. They were being killed simply because they were Jews.

As the soldiers pushed the women closer and closer to the river, a car suddenly pulled up onto the sidewalk. Out jumped a man, alone and unarmed. Walking up to the soldiers, he demanded that the women be released. Although the man was a stranger, the women knew instantly who he was. His name was Raoul Wallenberg. No one else in the world would dare to confront dozens of armed soldiers.

At first the soldiers refused to release the women. But Wallenberg did not give up. He announced that he represented the Swedish government. He said that the women were Swedish and were therefore under his protection. While Wallenberg was indeed a Swedish diplomat, he had no proof that the women were Swedish. In fact, that part of his story was a lie. The soldiers could easily have ignored him or simply shot him and left him to die in the street. But he acted with such confidence

and authority that the soldiers became frightened. After arguing with him for a few minutes, they backed down. Putting away their guns, they let the women go. Raoul Wallenberg had won another victory.

Most people who met Raoul Wallenberg were surprised to learn of his courageous battle against the Hungarian soldiers. After all, people said, Wallenberg certainly did not seem the heroic type. He was usually described as quiet, gentle and reserved. Some called him dreamy. Others thought he looked soft. Yet the young, rather weak-looking Swedish diplomat managed to save the lives of a hundred thousand Hungarian Jews during World War II.

Wallenberg arrived in Hungary in the summer of 1944. He had been appointed first secretary of the Swedish Embassy. While that was his official role, his real mission was to help the Jews still living in Hungary. His efforts were funded by America's War Refugee Board. He also had the complete support of Sweden's King Gustav.

Wallenberg took the job when he learned of the plight of the Hungarian Jews. In 1941, Hungary had entered World War II on the side of Nazi Germany. To Hungary, supporting Germany meant

more than just providing guns, soldiers and supplies. It also meant trying to wipe out all the Jews in the country. The extermination of all Jews was one of Adolf Hitler's main goals. And Hungary had embraced that goal with enthusiasm.

By July of 1944, over half a million Hungarian Jews had been imprisoned or killed. Only four hundred thousand remained. Most were living in the city of Budapest. Every day, more and more of them were being taken away to forced labor, torture and death. Although Wallenberg himself was not Jewish, he was outraged by what was happening. When he agreed to go to Hungary, he vowed to save the lives of as many Jews as he possibly could.

To accomplish his end, Wallenberg used every method available. He lodged formal protests with the government of Hungary. He bribed police officers. He used blackmail against certain high-ranking officials. And he handed out thousands of phony Swedish passports to Jews still living in Budapest.

Through such methods, Wallenberg was able to protect many Jews. But he could not stop all Nazi soldiers. The Hungarian government forced every Jew to wear a yellow star on his or her clothes. That made Jews easy targets for the cruel soldiers. Throughout the summer of 1944, Jews were packed into cattle cars and sent off to be killed in the gas chambers of concentration camps.

Later in the year, on October 20, the Hungarian soldiers staged a mass roundup of all Jewish men in the city. Although some escaped, over fifty thousand were hauled off to Nazi labor camps. There, many died from backbreaking work and inhumane treatment.

With most of the men gone, the soldiers turned their attention to the women. Starting on November 8, the Hungarian government authorized the first of several "death marches." Jewish women were dragged from their homes and forced to walk over a hundred miles to concentration camps. Conditions on the march were dreadful. The women had to walk up to twenty-five miles a day, sometimes in freezing rain. Anyone who fell behind was beaten and left to die. The women received no food or water along the way. At night they had to lie on the cold, hard ground with no blankets. Each night more and more of them froze to death.

When Wallenberg heard of the death marches, he was aghast. Seeing that his old methods were not enough to stop the marches, he resorted to bolder actions.

In Hungary, in the midst of World War II, the Nazis who were in power were rounding up all the Jews in the country and murdering them. When Raoul Wallenberg went to work in the embassy there, over half a million had already been killed. The quiet, gentle Swedish diplomat set out to save as many of the remaining Jews as he could. Without weapons, using formal protests, bribes and raw guts, he challenged the awful power of the Nazis. Though Wallenberg saved thousands of innocent people from death, his own fate became a mystery.

It was then that he began risking his life by confronting Hungarian soldiers face to face.

During those terrible November days, he traveled back and forth along the roads where the women were marching. He handed out food, medicine and warm clothing. Each time soldiers spotted him, they ordered him to stop. But he always ignored them. Often he stood at the side of the road handing out Swedish passports and writing down the names of women as they limped by. Then he would walk up to the officers in charge and show them his list of names. "These women are Swedish," he would say. "I demand that you let them go." Time after time he was able to frighten the officers with his forceful approach. Through his bravery, he managed to save over fifteen hundred women from certain death in the concentration camps. Through similar tactics, he was able to get fifteen thousand men released from Nazi labor camps.

By the end of 1944 it was clear that the Nazis were losing the war. Every day, Russian, American and European troops were gaining ground. The Russian army was moving closer and closer to Budapest. As a result, the Hungarian soldiers became more desperate and ruthless than ever. They conceived a plan to round up all the Jews in the city and kill them before the Russians arrived. They also wanted to find Wallenberg and kill him for all the trouble he had caused them.

Wallenberg's friends urged him to leave the city for his own safety, but he refused. He knew that the Jews were still in danger, so his work wasn't yet finished. By staying, Wallenberg was able to prevent the final massacre that the Nazis had planned. He did that by threatening the officers in charge of the roundup and by bribing hungry Hungarian soldiers with food supplies from the Swedish Embassy.

At last, in mid-January of 1945, the Russians arrived in Budapest. They drove out the Nazis and took over the city. Hungarian Jews were finally safe. While hundreds of thousands of them had died, 120,000 remained. Theirs was the only large Jewish community left in Europe. Most of the survivors owed their lives to Raoul Wallenberg.

The story of Raoul Wallenberg does not have a happy ending. For some unknown reason, the Russians accused him of being a Nazi spy. On January 17, 1945, they arrested him and took him to prison. He was never seen or heard from again. In the confusion that followed the war, Sweden did not immediately demand the return of its missing hero. By the time the Swedes did confront the Russians it was too late. The Russians claimed that Wallenberg had died of a heart attack in 1947.

It now appears that the Russians were lying. Russian prisoners who made their way to freedom reported having had contact with Wallenberg as late as 1959. Even in the late 1970s and early 1980s, the rumors continued. Released Russian prisoners told of a Swedish diplomat who had been in prison since the end of World War II. We will probably never know the truth about what happened to Raoul Wallenberg after January 17, 1945. But we do know that his efforts to save Hungarian Jews in 1944 make him one of the greatest heroes of all time. ■

If you have been timed while reading this selection, enter your reading time below. Then turn to the Words per Minute table on page 155 and look up your reading speed (words per minute). Enter your reading speed on the graph on page 156.

READING TIME: Unit 9

_____ : _____
Minutes   Seconds

How well did you read?

- *Answer the four types of questions that follow. The directions for each type of question tell you how to mark your answers.*

- *When you have finished all four exercises, check your work by using the answer key on page 151. For each right answer, put a check mark (✓) on the line beside the box. For each wrong answer, write the correct answer on the line.*

- *For scoring each exercise, follow the directions below the questions.*

A · FINDING THE MAIN IDEA

Look at the three statements below. One expresses the main idea of the story you just read. A good main idea statement answers two questions: it tells *who* or *what* is the subject of the story, and it answers the understood question *does what?* or *is what?* Another statement is *too broad,* it is vague and doesn't tell much about the topic of the story. The third statement is *too narrow,* it tells about only one part of the story.

Match the statements with the three answer choices below by writing the letter of each answer in the box in front of the statement it goes with.

M—Main Idea   B—Too Broad   N—Too Narrow

_____ ☐ 1. Raoul Wallenberg was a Swedish diplomat who hated what the Nazis stood for and worked to oppose them in Hungary during World War II.

_____ ☐ 2. Raoul Wallenberg regularly confronted Hungarian soldiers to save the lives of Jews who were going to be killed during World War II.

_____ ☐ 3. Raoul Wallenberg, a Swedish diplomat, risked his life to save a hundred thousand Hungarian Jews during World War II.

_____ Score 15 points for a correct *M* answer

_____ Score 5 points for each correct *B* or *N* answer

_____ TOTAL SCORE: Finding the Main Idea

B RECALLING FACTS

How well do you remember the facts in the story you just read? Put an x in the box in front of the correct answer to each of the multiple-choice questions below.

1. During World War II, all Jews in Hungary were forced to
   ____ ☐ a. wear yellow stars on their clothes.
   ____ ☐ b. work in labor camps.
   ____ ☐ c. sleep outside, even in freezing weather.

2. When Wallenberg agreed to go to Hungary, the number of Jews still alive in that country was
   ____ ☐ a. 50,000.
   ____ ☐ b. 120,000.
   ____ ☐ c. 400,000.

3. Wallenberg saved many Jews by claiming that they were
   ____ ☐ a. not really Jewish.
   ____ ☐ b. Swedish.
   ____ ☐ c. Nazis.

4. During the death marches, many women
   ____ ☐ a. escaped.
   ____ ☐ b. died of starvation.
   ____ ☐ c. froze to death.

5. On January 17, 1945, Raoul Wallenberg was arrested by
   ____ ☐ a. Hungarian soldiers.
   ____ ☐ b. Russian soldiers.
   ____ ☐ c. German soldiers.

Score 5 points for each correct answer

____ TOTAL SCORE: Recalling Facts

C MAKING INFERENCES

An inference is a judgment that is made or an idea that is arrived at based on facts or on information that is given. You make an inference when you understand something that is *not* stated directly, but that is *implied*, or suggested by the facts that are given.

Below are five statements that are judgments or ideas that have been arrived at from the facts of the story. Write the letter C in the box in front of each statement that is a correct inference. Write the letter F in front of each faulty inference.

C—Correct Inference   F—Faulty Inference

____ ☐ 1. Many of the Hungarian soldiers who gave in to Wallenberg were actually relieved to have an excuse for not having to murder innocent people.

____ ☐ 2. If Hitler's Germany had not started the extermination of the Jews, the Hungarian government would have.

____ ☐ 3. During World War II, Sweden was not at war with either Germany or Hungary.

____ ☐ 4. Wallenberg probably was a Nazi spy.

____ ☐ 5. Jews in other parts of Europe faced a fate similar to that of the Hungarian Jews.

Score 5 points for each correct answer

____ TOTAL SCORE: Making Inferences

D USING WORDS PRECISELY

Each of the numbered sentences below contains an underlined word or phrase from the story you have just read. Under the sentence are three definitions. One has the *same* meaning as the underlined word or phrase, one has *almost the same* meaning, and one has the *opposite* meaning. Match the definitions with the three answer choices by writing the letter that stands for each answer in the box in front of the definition it goes with.

S—Same   A—Almost the Same   O—Opposite

1. Wallenberg took the job when he learned of the <u>plight</u> of the Hungarian Jews.

   ____ ☐ a. difficulties

   ____ ☐ b. safe position

   ____ ☐ c. predicament

2. The <u>extermination</u> of the world's Jews was one of Adolf Hitler's main goals.

   ____ ☐ a. complete killing off

   ____ ☐ b. destruction

   ____ ☐ c. encouragement of development

3. And Hungary had <u>embraced</u> that goal with enthusiasm.

   ____ ☐ a. rejected

   ____ ☐ b. held

   ____ ☐ c. accepted

4. Starting on November 8, the Hungarian government <u>authorized</u> the first of several "death marches."

   ____ ☐ a. prohibited

   ____ ☐ b. allowed

   ____ ☐ c. formally ordered

5. As a result, the Hungarian soldiers became more desperate and <u>ruthless</u> than ever.

   ____ ☐ a. brutal

   ____ ☐ b. merciful

   ____ ☐ c. mean

____ Score 3 points for each correct S answer
____ Score 1 point for each correct A or O answer

____ TOTAL SCORE: Using Words Precisely

● *Enter the four total scores in the spaces below, and add them together to find your Critical Reading Score. Then record your Critical Reading Score on the graph on page 157.*

_____	Finding the Main Idea
_____	Recalling Facts
_____	Making Inferences
_____	Using Words Precisely
_____	CRITICAL READING SCORE: Unit 9

Anne and Charles Lindbergh: Opening the Skies

He was the most famous person in the world. She was the daughter of the American ambassador to Mexico. In 1927 he became the first pilot to fly nonstop across the Atlantic Ocean, traveling from New York to Paris. She knew nothing about airplanes or flying. He loved cars, planes—anything that went fast. She loved books and hoped one day to become a writer. Charles and Anne Lindbergh seemed to have little in common. Yet together they wrote some of the most important pages in the history of aviation.

Anne and Charles married in 1929. Charles made it clear from the beginning that he did not want his wife to sit at home while he was off flying. If they were going to be married, they were going to be a team. Anne would have to learn to use Morse Code and to operate a two-way radio. She would also have to learn how to navigate. She did all of that gladly. Wherever Charles decided to fly, Anne was prepared to be right there in the cockpit with him.

In 1931 the Lindberghs got their first big opportunity to work together. Charles, who was a technical consultant for Pan American Airways, was contacted by Juan Trippe, the company's founder. Trippe asked the Lindberghs to survey an air route from the United States to Asia. The route was a great circle route. A great circle route is the shortest distance between two points on the earth's surface. This particular route ran over Canada, across Alaska, and down to Japan and China. It was the shortest distance between the east coast of North America and the Orient.

No one had ever flown the route before, and many pilots doubted that it could be done. Pilots familiar with the Arctic urged Charles and Anne not to try it. They pointed out the dangerous weather conditions that prevailed along the route. Storms and fog sprang up without warning. There were no landing strips, supply stations or refueling pads along the way. For much of the trip the Lindberghs would be out of radio contact with the rest of the world. And near the North Pole, the pull from the magnetic pole would make their compass worthless.

The Lindberghs listened as the pilots ran down the list of dangers. But in the end they decided to make the attempt anyway. Charles, eager for new challenges, believed that if they planned the trip carefully enough they could make it. Once that decision was made, he and Anne began preparing for the journey.

To begin with, they bought the best plane available. It was a seaplane, which meant it was equipped with pontoons for water landings. With a top speed of 185 miles per hour, it was one of the fastest planes of its day. When the Lindberghs saw the plane, they decided to name it *Sirius*, after the brightest star in the sky.

The sleek black and red *Sirius* could carry enough gasoline to travel two thousand miles. The total mileage of the trip, however, was more than eight thousand miles. The Lindberghs, therefore, had to arrange for fuel tanks to be set out along the route. Next they had to decide what supplies to take with them. They packed repair kits and emergency medical supplies. They took parachutes in case they had to abandon the plane. They packed handguns so they could shoot animals if they ran out of food. They brought along matches, rope and a rubber raft. They even packed special flight suits that could be heated by electricity to ward off the Arctic cold.

By July 29, 1931, the Lindberghs were ready. They took off from College Point, Long Island, in New York, to Maine, where they stopped briefly to visit family. From there they went to Ottawa, Canada. On August 1 they left Ottawa and started northwest across the continent. The first part of the trip went smoothly. With Charles at the controls and Anne working the radio, they made good progress. Each day they flew farther and farther north.

Each night they landed on a river or lake and dropped anchor. For the first week it seemed that all the dangers they had been warned about were imaginary. But on August 8, as they approached Point Barrow in northern Alaska, things began to go wrong.

First they hit a fog so dense that they could see nothing but fine white mist all around them. They managed to land safely at Point Barrow, but there they found bad news awaiting them. The gasoline they had ordered had not yet reached the tiny coastal town. They had no way to refuel. After discussing the situation, Anne and Charles decided to keep going, rather than wait for the fuel to reach them. Charles figured the *Sirius* had just enough fuel left to make it to Nome, Alaska.

On the afternoon of August 11, the Lindberghs left Point Barrow and headed southwest toward the small mining town of Nome. They expected it would take about seven hours to get there. Ordinarily they would not have left so late in the day. They didn't want to get caught flying at night over unfamiliar territory. But this time they did not worry. It was summertime and they were in the Arctic. They were sure that the summer sun never set in that part of the world.

But Charles and Anne were wrong

In the early 1930s, flying as a means of travel was just beginning to gain popularity. The decade was to bring many innovations to aviation, including new, sleek aircraft specially designed to carry people, and air routes that connected the far corners of the earth. The new routes were pioneered by adventuresome flyers who were willing to risk traveling over uncharted areas, surveying the land and finding the most suitable places for airfields. Anne and Charles Lindbergh were among the most talented and daring of those pioneering aviators. In 1931, they surveyed the route from New York to China that is marked on this map. The flight took them through the treacherous cold and wilderness of the Arctic, over one of the most dangerous courses ever flown.

about the sun. It was true that the Arctic sky never got very dark in June. But this was August. Besides, the Lindberghs were flying south, away from the land of endless summer light. By 8:00 P.M. it was clear that the sun *was* going down. By 8:30 it had gotten so dark that Anne could barely read the note her husband handed her. The message read, "What time does it get dark in Nome?"

Quickly Anne went to work on the radio. She had to contact Nome. She needed to find out if there would be enough daylight left for them to land on the Nome River as planned. They were still almost two hours from Nome, and the *Sirius* was running low on gas. They didn't have the time or the fuel to look for another landing spot.

The radio operator in Nome sent back a message that was not encouraging. It was already getting dark there. The radio operator offered to put flares out along the Nome River, but still the Lindberghs would be landing in the dark.

Both Charles and Anne knew that they should not do that. It was simply too dangerous. They didn't know the exact width, depth or contour of the river. If they tried to land there in the dark, they might injure themselves or the plane.

They decided to make a forced landing somewhere and wait until morning to fly into Nome. They had to hurry; it was getting darker every second. Anne radioed Nome to tell the radio operator their plan. Then Charles sent the plane plunging through the clouds and mist toward an ocean inlet. Somehow he managed to land the *Sirius* safely in the small patch of calm water. Not until the plane had landed did the Lindberghs realize the water in the inlet was only three feet deep.

The next morning, recovered from their close call, Charles and Anne continued their journey. They stopped briefly in Nome to refuel the *Sirius*. As they traveled farther along their course, they ran into many other frightening situations. At one point the fog became incredibly thick. In order to see anything at all, they had to fly up and down the sides of mountains, very close to treetops and rocky ledges. Terrified, Anne felt sure they were going to crash. To her, it seemed the plane had suddenly become "like a knife going down the side of a pie tin, between fog and mountains." At another point, bad weather forced them to fly so low that the *Sirius* actually did skip across the treetops. In the course of the trip, they made three emergency landings.

Despite all the difficulties, however, on September 19, 1931, the Lindberghs landed in China. That ended their long and dangerous journey. They had successfully flown where no one else had dared to go. They had proved that it was possible to fly the great circle route from New York to the Orient. In the years that followed, the Lindberghs went on to pioneer other air routes. By the time their flying careers ended, Charles and Anne Lindbergh had changed the way people looked at aviation. ■

If you have been timed while reading this selection, enter your reading time below. Then turn to the Words per Minute table on page 155 and look up your reading speed (words per minute). Enter your reading speed on the graph on page 156.

READING TIME: Unit 10

_____ : _____
Minutes   *Seconds*

How well did you read?

- *Answer the four types of questions that follow. The directions for each type of question tell you how to mark your answers.*

- *When you have finished all four exercises, check your work by using the answer key on page 151. For each right answer, put a check mark (✔) on the line beside the box. For each wrong answer, write the correct answer on the line.*

- *For scoring each exercise, follow the directions below the questions.*

A FINDING THE MAIN IDEA

Look at the three statements below. One expresses the main idea of the story you just read. A good main idea statement answers two questions: it tells *who* or *what* is the subject of the story, and it answers the understood question *does what?* or *is what?* Another statement is *too broad*, it is vague and doesn't tell much about the topic of the story. The third statement is *too narrow*, it tells about only one part of the story.

Match the statements with the three answer choices below by writing the letter of each answer in the box in front of the statement it goes with.

M—Main Idea   **B—Too Broad**   **N—Too Narrow**

____ ☐ 1. Charles and Anne Lindbergh met with great difficulties as they flew across Alaska.

____ ☐ 2. Charles and Anne Lindbergh were among the world's greatest aviation pioneers.

____ ☐ 3. Charles and Anne Lindbergh were the first aviators to fly the dangerous great circle route from New York to the Orient.

____ Score 15 points for a correct *M* answer

____ Score 5 points for each correct *B* or *N* answer

____ TOTAL SCORE: Finding the Main Idea

B RECALLING FACTS

How well do you remember the facts in the story you just read? Put an *x* in the box in front of the correct answer to each of the multiple-choice questions below.

1. Anne Lindbergh's early desire was to become a
____ ☐ a. pilot.
____ ☐ b. radio operator.
____ ☐ c. writer.

2. *Sirius,* the Lindberghs' plane, was named after
____ ☐ a. the brightest star in the sky.
____ ☐ b. a city in China.
____ ☐ c. the founder of Pan American Airways.

3. The Lindberghs were running out of both gas and daylight on their way to
____ ☐ a. Nome, Alaska.
____ ☐ b. Point Barrow, Alaska.
____ ☐ c. Ottawa, Canada.

4. The greatest danger the Lindberghs faced while flying to Nome was
____ ☐ a. an Arctic storm.
____ ☐ b. approaching darkness.
____ ☐ c. a useless compass.

5. The ocean inlet that the Lindberghs were forced to land on was only
____ ☐ a. three inches deep.
____ ☐ b. three feet deep.
____ ☐ c. six inches deep.

Score 5 points for each correct answer

____ TOTAL SCORE: Recalling Facts

C MAKING INFERENCES

An inference is a judgment that is made or an idea that is arrived at based on facts or on information that is given. You make an inference when you understand something that is *not* stated directly, but that is *implied,* or suggested by the facts that are given.

Below are five statements that are judgments or ideas that have been arrived at from the facts of the story. Write the letter *C* in the box in front of each statement that is a correct inference. Write the letter *F* in front of each faulty inference.

C—Correct Inference   F—Faulty Inference

____ ☐ 1. Anne Lindbergh would not have become an important pioneer in aviation if she had not married Charles Lindbergh.

____ ☐ 2. The survey of the great circle route from New York to China was the first dangerous flight Charles Lindbergh had ever made.

____ ☐ 3. The Lindberghs would not have found themselves in such dangerous situations if they had planned their trip more carefully.

____ ☐ 4. The Lindberghs' flight from New York to the Orient helped to open up the skies for the growing business of aviation.

____ ☐ 5. The great circle route across the Arctic is still a difficult and dangerous route to fly.

Score 5 points for each correct answer

____ TOTAL SCORE: Making Inferences

D USING WORDS PRECISELY

Each of the numbered sentences below contains an underlined word or phrase from the story you have just read. Under the sentence are three definitions. One has the *same* meaning as the underlined word or phrase, one has *almost the same* meaning, and one has the *opposite* meaning. Match the definitions with the three answer choices by writing the letter that stands for each answer in the box in front of the definition it goes with.

S—Same   A—Almost the Same   O—Opposite

1. Trippe asked the Lindberghs to <u>survey</u> an air route from the United States to Asia.

____ ☐ a. look at

____ ☐ b. avoid

____ ☐ c. explore

2. Charles, <u>eager</u> for new challenges, believed that if they planned the trip carefully enough, they could make it.

____ ☐ a. wanting greatly

____ ☐ b. accepting

____ ☐ c. avoiding

3. They even packed special flight suits heated by electricity to <u>ward off</u> the Arctic cold.

____ ☐ a. attract

____ ☐ b. protect against

____ ☐ c. control

4. They decided to make a <u>forced</u> landing somewhere and wait until morning to fly into Nome.

____ ☐ a. involuntary

____ ☐ b. planned

____ ☐ c. required

5. Then Charles sent the plane <u>plunging</u> through the clouds and mist toward an ocean inlet.

____ ☐ a. descending

____ ☐ b. diving headlong

____ ☐ c. rising straight up

____ Score 3 points for each correct S answer
____ Score 1 point for each correct A or O answer

____ TOTAL SCORE: Using Words Precisely

- *Enter the four total scores in the spaces below, and add them together to find your Critical Reading Score. Then record your Critical Reading Score on the graph on page 157.*

_____	Finding the Main Idea
_____	Recalling Facts
_____	Making Inferences
_____	Using Words Precisely
_____	CRITICAL READING SCORE: Unit 10

Yonatan Netanyahu was an unusual person with many strengths. He had a quick and brilliant mind that loved learning. He was devoted to his family and his country. He was one of the finest officers in the Israeli army. He loved life, and he had a lot to live for. Yet, when his country's leaders asked him to plan and lead an extremely dangerous mission to rescue 105 hostages from a group of terrorists, Yoni paused for only a moment before accepting the challenge.

Yoni Netanyahu: The Impossible Rescue

Yonatan Netanyahu hated to leave Harvard University. He loved the history, philosophy and literature he had been studying there. His professors told him he had a brilliant mind and encouraged him to stay. But Yonatan, or Yoni, as his friends called him, knew he had to leave. He felt it was his duty to return to Israel. His country was being threatened by nearby Arab states; it needed young men to serve in its army.

On June 2, 1968, Yoni returned to Israel and signed up for military service. His good judgment, self-discipline and sense of fairness made him an excellent officer. For the next few years he led his troops in battle. He became one of the best officers in the Israeli army. He often fought against Arab terrorists. Terrorists are groups that use terror—such things as bombings and killings—to accomplish their goals. Arab terrorists wanted to destroy the state of Israel and regain land they claimed Israel had stolen from the Arab people. Yoni believed that terrorists were the worst kind of outlaws. He longed for a chance to show the world that Israel would not tolerate them.

That chance came on Thursday, July 1, 1976, when Yoni received an urgent message from the leaders of the Israeli government. They wanted to meet with him right away. They needed to talk to him about a grave situation. Although it was late at night, Yoni rushed to the army base in the city of Tel Aviv. He was asked to lead a rescue mission into the African country of Uganda. A hundred and five people were being held hostage there by pro-Arab terrorists.

The hostages, most of them Israeli citizens, had been flying from Tel Aviv to Paris, France. Halfway through the flight, the terrorists had hijacked the plane. They had forced the pilot to land at Entebbe Airport in Uganda. Uganda had been chosen because it was controlled by a madman named Idi Amin. Amin offered protection to the terrorists. He even agreed to send some of his own soldiers to the airport to help guard the hostages.

The hijackers demanded the release of fifty-three terrorists who had been captured and imprisoned. Most of them were in Israeli jails. The hijackers threatened to begin killing the hostages if their demand was not met by July 4. The Israelis did not want to give in to the terrorists. Their only other option, however, was a military rescue of the hostages. That was why they had sent for Yoni; they needed to find out if such a rescue was possible.

As Yoni studied the proposed mission, he realized the tremendous risks involved.

Uganda was more than two thousand miles away. To accomplish a rescue, Israel would need to send planes with commando troops. The planes would have to sneak past Ugandan radar. The troops would then have to get past dozens of Ugandan soldiers stationed around the airport. They would have to break into the main building and kill the seven terrorists without being killed themselves. Finally, they would have to load the hostages onto the planes and get out of Uganda alive. It seemed like an impossible task.

When asked if he would lead the mission, Yoni hesitated. He recognized that the slightest mistake in planning or action could be fatal. He wondered if he was up to the challenge. But he also realized the importance of attempting the rescue. Israel could not just knuckle under to the terrorists. Few Israeli officers had as much experience with terrorists as he had. If he didn't agree to lead the mission, his government might be forced to meet the hijackers' demands. With that thought in mind, Yoni agreed to accept the assignment.

He spent the rest of the night mapping out the details of the rescue attempt. Then, after resting for an hour, he called his troops together and began preparing them for the mission. By Saturday, July 3, they were ready to go. That afternoon they boarded three jets and took off for Entebbe Airport.

As the planes approached Uganda, they flew close to the ground to escape Ugandan radar. At times they flew a mere fifty feet above the earth. Just before midnight, they reached Entebbe Airport. After landing, Yoni and his men jumped out of the planes. Because of Yoni's careful instructions, the men knew exactly what to do. They split into three groups and headed for the main building. Two of the groups were to attack the Ugandan guards. Their goal was to wound them or cause them to flee, not to kill them. The other group, led by Yoni, had responsibility for confronting the terrorists.

As the three groups moved in, the Ugandan guards tried to stop them. But the Israelis shot them down and kept running. When they reached the main building, they burst into the lobby. The hostages were lying on the floor, half asleep. The terrorists stood nearby, holding pistols and machine guns, but they had been caught completely by surprise. Before they could react, Yoni and his troops opened fire.

Yoni then headed back outside. He wanted to make sure that no Ugandan guards were left in the area. As he stepped outside, a guard jumped out of the darkness. One of Yoni's men quickly shot him, but before the guard dropped, he managed to get off a short burst of machine-gun fire. One of the bullets hit Yoni, who spun and fell to the ground. His men tried to stop the bleeding as they rushed him back to an Israeli plane. There a doctor took over, but it was too late. Yonatan Netanyahu was dead.

Meanwhile, the other troops ushered the frightened hostages to the waiting planes. Three of the hostages had been wounded in the raid and later died. But the other 102 survived and were carried safely back to Israel.

When news of the rescue reached Israel, the entire country burst into celebration. Hundreds of people gathered at the airport in Tel Aviv. They welcomed the hostages and cheered the brave commando troops. One of the most daring rescues ever attempted had been a great success. Israel had struck a blow against terrorism that was felt around the world.

The jubilation of the Israeli people was tempered only by the knowledge that Yoni Netanyahu was dead. Everyone knew that without him the mission might never have taken place. They knew that it was his calm, brave spirit that had inspired his men. So even as they celebrated, they mourned the death of the gentle, scholarly man who had given up his life for a noble cause. ■

If you have been timed while reading this selection, enter your reading time below. Then turn to the Words per Minute table on page 155 and look up your reading speed (words per minute). Enter your reading speed on the graph on page 156.

READING TIME: Unit 11

_____ : _____

Minutes   Seconds

How well did you read?

- *Answer the four types of questions that follow. The directions for each type of question tell you how to mark your answers.*

- *When you have finished all four exercises, check your work by using the answer key on page 151. For each right answer, put a check mark (✔) on the line beside the box. For each wrong answer, write the correct answer on the line.*

- *For scoring each exercise, follow the directions below the questions.*

A FINDING THE MAIN IDEA

Look at the three statements below. One expresses the main idea of the story you just read. A good main idea statement answers two questions: it tells *who* or *what* is the subject of the story, and it answers the understood question *does what?* or *is what?* Another statement is *too broad,* it is vague and doesn't tell much about the topic of the story. The third statement is *too narrow,* it tells about only one part of the story.

Match the statements with the three answer choices below by writing the letter of each answer in the box in front of the statement it goes with.

M—Main Idea   **B—Too Broad**   **N—Too Narrow**

_____ ☐ 1. Yoni Netanyahu lost his life in a brave and daring rescue of 105 hostages held captive at Entebbe Airport.

_____ ☐ 2. When Yoni Netanyahu stepped outside the main building at Entebbe Airport in Uganda, he was killed by a Ugandan soldier.

_____ ☐ 3. Yoni Netanyahu was a brave and dedicated Israeli soldier who will always be remembered by the people of Israel.

_____ Score 15 points for a correct *M* answer

_____ Score 5 points for each correct *B* or *N* answer

_____ TOTAL SCORE: Finding the Main Idea

B RECALLING FACTS

How well do you remember the facts in the story you just read? Put an *x* in the box in front of the correct answer to each of the multiple-choice questions below.

1. The hijackers demanded
   - ____ ☐ a. the release of fifty-three imprisoned terrorists.
   - ____ ☐ b. a meeting with Idi Amin.
   - ____ ☐ c. a plane that would take them from Uganda to Paris, France.

2. Yoni left Harvard University because
   - ____ ☐ a. he wanted a career in the army.
   - ____ ☐ b. he was tired of studying philosophy and history.
   - ____ ☐ c. he felt he had a duty to fight for his country.

3. Idi Amin was
   - ____ ☐ a. a leader in the Israeli government.
   - ____ ☐ b. a pro-Arab terrorist.
   - ____ ☐ c. the leader of Uganda.

4. As the Israeli planes approached Uganda, they flew close to the ground in order to
   - ____ ☐ a. better see Entebbe Airport.
   - ____ ☐ b. escape Ugandan radar.
   - ____ ☐ c. count the number of Ugandan soldiers stationed at Entebbe Airport.

5. As a result of the rescue raid,
   - ____ ☐ a. all the hostages were returned safely.
   - ____ ☐ b. three hostages died, but 102 were saved.
   - ____ ☐ c. three hostages died, but 53 were saved.

Score 5 points for each correct answer

____ TOTAL SCORE: Recalling Facts

C MAKING INFERENCES

An inference is a judgment that is made or an idea that is arrived at based on facts or on information that is given. You make an inference when you understand something that is *not* stated directly, but that is *implied*, or suggested by the facts that are given.

Below are five statements that are judgments or ideas that have been arrived at from the facts of the story. Write the letter C in the box in front of each statement that is a correct inference. Write the letter F in front of each faulty inference.

C—Correct Inference   F—Faulty Inference

- ____ ☐ 1. The terrorists thought that Israel might agree to their demands.
- ____ ☐ 2. Most countries would not have offered help and protection to the hijackers.
- ____ ☐ 3. The Israeli government had a great deal of faith in Yoni Netanyahu.
- ____ ☐ 4. If Yoni had lived, he would have become a top government official in Israel.
- ____ ☐ 5. The Israelis would not have attempted to rescue the hostages if they thought that anybody would die in the attack.

Score 5 points for each correct answer

____ TOTAL SCORE: Making Inferences

D USING WORDS PRECISELY

Each of the numbered sentences below contains an underlined word or phrase from the story you have just read. Under the sentence are three definitions. One has the *same* meaning as the underlined word or phrase, one has *almost the same* meaning, and one has the *opposite* meaning. Match the definitions with the three answer choices by writing the letter that stands for each answer in the box in front of the definition it goes with.

S—Same   A—Almost the Same   O—Opposite

1. He longed for a chance to show the world that Israel would not <u>tolerate</u> them.

____ ☐ a. hold out against

____ ☐ b. put up with

____ ☐ c. accept

2. At the same time, however, he did not want to see Israel <u>knuckle under</u> to the hijackers.

____ ☐ a. compromise

____ ☐ b. stand up to

____ ☐ c. surrender

3. The other group, led by Yoni, had responsibility for <u>confronting</u> the terrorists.

____ ☐ a. avoiding

____ ☐ b. facing

____ ☐ c. seeing

4. Meanwhile, the other troops <u>ushered</u> the frightened hostages to the waiting planes.

____ ☐ a. accompanied

____ ☐ b. followed

____ ☐ c. led

5. The jubilation of the Israeli people was <u>tempered</u> only by the knowledge that Yoni Netanyahu was dead.

____ ☐ a. toned down

____ ☐ b. altered

____ ☐ c. increased

____ Score 3 points for each correct S answer
____ Score 1 point for each correct A or O answer

____ TOTAL SCORE: Using Words Precisely

● *Enter the four total scores in the spaces below, and add them together to find your Critical Reading Score. Then record your Critical Reading Score on the graph on page 157.*

_____ Finding the Main Idea
_____ Recalling Facts
_____ Making Inferences
_____ Using Words Precisely

_____ CRITICAL READING SCORE: Unit 11

Steve Biko: South African Freedom Fighter

Twenty thousand blacks jammed the streets of King William's Town, South Africa. They had come to pay their last respects to the great black leader Steve Biko. Many wept as an ox cart moved through the streets, carrying his coffin to the graveyard. Then, as the coffin was lowered into the ground, the mourners raised their right fists in a show of unity. They pledged to continue the battle Steve had fought. They vowed to win freedom and equality for the blacks of South Africa. All across the country, millions of other blacks echoed that pledge.

Steve Biko had not been the only person fighting for the rights of blacks in South Africa. But from 1967 until his death in 1977, he had been the undisputed leader of that struggle. His political career began at the age of twenty, when he decided that he could no longer tolerate the laws of his racist society. Everywhere he and his fellow blacks went, they were treated like dirt.

Despite the fact that there are four times as many blacks as whites in the Republic of South Africa, whites have controlled the government for well over a hundred years. To make sure that they could maintain control, they made and enforced laws that kept blacks from having any power. They went to such extremes, in fact, that they kept the black population from having even the most basic civil and human rights.

Steve Biko wanted to help change the laws that oppressed the native people of South Africa. Those laws did not allow blacks to vote. They kept them from living in the capital city. They forbade them from using the same elevators, beaches and toilets as whites. Blacks were not even allowed to move from one town to another to look for work.

In an effort to change the laws that prevented blacks from being full members of society, Steve Biko founded a movement called Black Consciousness. The purpose of the movement was to build a sense of pride among the blacks of South Africa. Steve wanted to teach them that they were just as good as whites. They had been oppressed for so long that many had grown to believe that they were in fact inferior. Steve knew that if his people gained confidence and joined together they could change the racist laws of South Africa. Like Martin Luther King, Jr., in the United States, he opposed the use of violence. He hoped to change the society through peaceful means.

To awaken the spirits of his people, Steve wrote pamphlets and delivered speeches. He spoke out against the racist policies of the government. He condemned the white policemen who beat black citizens for no reason. He attacked the rich whites who forced blacks to live in poverty, often on the verge of starvation. But most importantly, he called on blacks to stand up for their basic human rights.

Because of Steve Biko's work, the Black Consciousness movement spread quickly. Other groups soon sprang up to advance the cause of black pride and racial equality. The largest of the new groups were the Black Peoples' Convention and the all-black South African Students' Organization. The heads of the groups were all dedicated and courageous people. But even to them, Steve was special. They saw him as one of the most inspiring leaders South Africa had ever known.

As the Black Consciousness movement grew, government officials became worried. They feared that they might lose control of the country. To prevent that, they ordered the police to begin arresting black leaders. From 1967 to 1977, hundreds of black activists were jailed. Many were kept in prisons for months without trial. Some were never even charged with committing a crime. The prisoners often suffered beatings by white guards. In thirty-five cases, guards actually beat black prisoners to death.

As Steve Biko's popularity grew, the South African police zeroed in on him. In 1973 they banned his leaflets and ordered him not to make any more speeches. They declared that he could not be quoted and that he could not be in a room with more than one person at a time. They also ordered him to stay within the boundaries of his home town. Finally, they warned him that the security police would be watching his every move. His phone was tapped. The police kept track of all his visitors. And whenever they felt like it, they entered and searched his home.

All those measures were meant to keep Steve Biko out of the public spotlight. If he could not communicate with anyone, he could not stir the people to action.

But Steve was not willing to quit. Despite the ban, he kept writing pamphlets. He had them smuggled to underground presses and printed without his name on them. With the help of friends and supporters, he was able to travel outside his town. Speaking in a special code, he continued to use the telephone. So in many ways, Steve continued to provide leadership for the Black Consciousness movement. In addition, he kept up his contacts with other black leaders. Since he could not attend public meetings, he invited members

Steve Biko spoke out against the injustices done to his people—the blacks of South Africa. He wanted to change the laws that humiliated them and kept them poor and downtrodden in a society in which they formed the majority. The white government feared and hated him. Officials knew that he held great influence, and they were threatened by him. In their fear, they tried to keep him silent. But Steve Biko found ways to keep talking and to keep encouraging hope, pride and unity in his people.

of black activist groups to his home one at a time. He gave them advice and encouragement. People were soon traveling from all over South Africa and from many foreign countries for private talks with Steve Biko.

Steve knew the risks of disobeying the government. If caught, he would almost certainly spend the rest of his life in jail. But that didn't matter. He had to continue the fight. He felt that the work he was doing was more important than his personal safety. He was prepared to pay any price in the battle to wipe out racial injustice.

If Steve Biko didn't give up, however, neither did the South African government. Acting on orders from top officials, the security police arrested Steve twenty times. Each time, they tried to prove that he had committed a crime. But they always had to release him for lack of evidence. The police also repeatedly raided Steve's home. They hoped to catch him breaking an order, but they never succeeded. Often some of Steve's friends acted as lookouts and warned him when the police were coming. Other times, when he was taken by surprise, Steve managed to stall the police while his wife hid illegal papers and pamphlets.

Finally the police had had enough. They decided to get rid of Steve Biko one way or another. On August 18, 1977, they arrested him and took him to head-quarters. They did not charge him with any crime. They simply forced him out of his car and dragged him to jail. They stripped him of his clothes and put him in leg irons. He remained chained to a wall for several days, while the leg irons cut into his ankles. Then the police hauled him off to be questioned.

They grilled him for hours at a time, trying to get him to confess to all sorts of crimes. When he continually refused to cooperate, they began beating him. They struck him over and over again on the head. After the brutal beating, Steve showed many signs of brain damage. But the signs were ignored until it was too late. On September 12, 1977, while still in police custody, Steve Biko died.

The news of Steve's death shocked the entire black community. In response to demands from other black leaders, the South African government reluctantly agreed to conduct an inquiry. At the hearing, ample evidence was presented of police brutality and neglect. Despite the evidence, however, all police officers and government officials were found innocent.

South Africa is still an oppressive and racist society. The white leaders of the country still refuse to grant blacks their basic human rights. So the struggle continues. Although Steve Biko is dead, his memory lives. His message of non-violent protest and black unity continues to inspire new black leaders. Through his courage, inner strength and personal sacrifice, he set an example for all people to follow. ∎

If you have been timed while reading this selection, enter your reading time below. Then turn to the Words per Minute table on page 155 and look up your reading speed (words per minute). Enter your reading speed on the graph on page 156.

READING TIME: Unit 12
_____ : _____
Minutes   _Seconds_

How well did you read?

- *Answer the four types of questions that follow. The directions for each type of question tell you how to mark your answers.*

- *When you have finished all four exercises, check your work by using the answer key on page 151. For each right answer, put a check mark (✔) on the line beside the box. For each wrong answer, write the correct answer on the line.*

- *For scoring each exercise, follow the directions below the questions.*

A FINDING THE MAIN IDEA

Look at the three statements below. One expresses the main idea of the story you just read. A good main idea statement answers two questions: it tells *who* or *what* is the subject of the story, and it answers the understood question *does what?* or *is what?* Another statement is *too broad*, it is vague and doesn't tell much about the topic of the story. The third statement is *too narrow*, it tells about only one part of the story.

Match the statements with the three answer choices below by writing the letter of each answer in the box in front of the statement it goes with.

M—Main Idea   B—Too Broad   N—Too Narrow

_____ ☐ 1. Steve Biko was committed to trying to win rights for blacks in South Africa.

_____ ☐ 2. Steve Biko died after he was beaten by South African police during a questioning session.

_____ ☐ 3. Steve Biko sacrificed his life in an effort to win racial equality for blacks in South Africa.

_____ Score 15 points for a correct *M* answer

_____ Score 5 points for each correct *B* or *N* answer

_____ TOTAL SCORE: Finding the Main Idea

B RECALLING FACTS

How well do you remember the facts in the story you just read?
Put an x in the box in front of the correct answer to each of the
multiple-choice questions below.

1. In South Africa no black could
   - ____ ☐ a. write pamphlets.
   - ____ ☐ b. vote.
   - ____ ☐ c. be with more than one person at a time.

2. Steve Biko wanted blacks to
   - ____ ☐ a. develop a sense of pride.
   - ____ ☐ b. fight back when police beat them.
   - ____ ☐ c. use violence to change South African racial
     policy.

3. Steve disobeyed the government's orders because
   - ____ ☐ a. he didn't think he would be caught.
   - ____ ☐ b. he didn't think the police would put him in
     jail for very long.
   - ____ ☐ c. he felt his work was too important to be
     stopped.

4. When Steve was arrested on August 18, 1977, he
   - ____ ☐ a. immediately confessed to going against the
     government's orders.
   - ____ ☐ b. used a special code to telephone his family.
   - ____ ☐ c. was stripped of his clothes and put in chains.

5. As a result of the investigation into Steve Biko's death,
   - ____ ☐ a. policy toward blacks began to change.
   - ____ ☐ b. neither the government nor the police were
     found guilty.
   - ____ ☐ c. the police were found guilty of brutality.

Score 5 points for each correct answer

____ TOTAL SCORE: Recalling Facts

C MAKING INFERENCES

An inference is a judgment that is made or an idea that is
arrived at based on facts or on information that is given. You
make an inference when you understand something that is *not*
stated directly, but that is *implied*, or suggested by the facts that
are given.

Below are five statements that are judgments or ideas that
have been arrived at from the facts of the story. Write the letter
C in the box in front of each statement that is a correct inference. Write the letter F in front of each faulty inference.

C—Correct Inference   **F—Faulty Inference**

- ____ ☐ 1. If the blacks in South Africa were allowed to vote
  and to hold political office, whites would still
  rule the country.

- ____ ☐ 2. If Steve Biko had lived longer, sooner or later he
  would have turned to violent means to change
  South Africa's racial policies.

- ____ ☐ 3. The South African government feared that Steve's
  speeches and pamphlets would stir up trouble
  among blacks.

- ____ ☐ 4. Steve Biko did not have many friends.

- ____ ☐ 5. South African police did not beat white prisoners
  the way they beat black prisoners.

Score 5 points for each correct answer

____ TOTAL SCORE: Making Inferences

D USING WORDS PRECISELY

Each of the numbered sentences below contains an underlined word or phrase from the story you have just read. Under the sentence are three definitions. One has the *same* meaning as the underlined word or phrase, one has *almost the same* meaning, and one has the *opposite* meaning. Match the definitions with the three answer choices by writing the letter that stands for each answer in the box in front of the definition it goes with.

S—Same   A—Almost the Same   O—Opposite

1. Blacks had been oppressed for so long that many had grown to believe that they were in fact inferior.

____ ☐ a. abused

____ ☐ b. assisted

____ ☐ c. kept down

2. He attacked the rich whites who forced blacks to live in poverty, often on the verge of starvation.

____ ☐ a. bordering

____ ☐ b. far from

____ ☐ c. near

3. He was prepared to pay any price in the battle to wipe out racial injustice.

____ ☐ a. foul play

____ ☐ b. unfairness

____ ☐ c. equality

4. In response to demands from other black leaders, the South African government reluctantly agreed to conduct an inquiry.

____ ☐ a. enthusiastically

____ ☐ b. unwillingly

____ ☐ c. unhappily

5. At the hearing there was ample evidence of police brutality and neglect.

____ ☐ a. plenty of

____ ☐ b. not enough

____ ☐ c. quite a lot of

____ Score 3 points for each correct *S* answer
____ Score 1 point for each correct *A* or *O* answer

____ TOTAL SCORE: Using Words Precisely

● *Enter the four total scores in the spaces below, and add them together to find your Critical Reading Score. Then record your Critical Reading Score on the graph on page 157.*

_____ Finding the Main Idea
_____ Recalling Facts
_____ Making Inferences
_____ Using Words Precisely

_____ CRITICAL READING SCORE: Unit 12

Ten thousand national guardsmen to protect nine high school students and escort them into their school and to their classes? What could the kids have done to need such protection? They were the first black students to try to attend the all-white high school in Little Rock, Arkansas.

The Little Rock Nine

Fifteen-year-old Elizabeth Eckford hurried to get ready for school. After putting on the new dress she had made, she grabbed her notebook and headed out the door. On the way to the city bus stop, she said a prayer. She wasn't afraid, but she was a little nervous. It was Wednesday, September 4, 1957, and she was on her way to Central High School in Little Rock, Arkansas. She and eight other teenagers were about to become the first blacks ever to attend that all-white school.

A federal court had ordered Central High to begin admitting black students. Three years earlier, in 1954, the United States Supreme Court had ruled that it was unconstitutional to require blacks and whites to go to separate public schools. Such a system did not offer equal educational opportunities for everyone. Hundreds of schools had become partially integrated since 1954. But in spite of the Supreme Court ruling, Arkansas had not yet begun to integrate its schools. The order to Central High to open its doors to blacks was an order for the state to begin the process of desegregation.

The bus dropped Elizabeth off one block from Central High. As she walked toward the school, she saw hundreds of white people surrounding the building. She also saw members of the Arkansas National Guard standing by the doorways. The guardsmen were holding rifles equipped with bayonets. Elizabeth assumed that the soldiers were there to protect her. She thought they would help her get into the school and make sure no one in the crowd bothered her.

As she approached the school, she tried not to notice the people staring at her. Still, she sensed their anger. She knew those people hated her. They hated her because of her color. They didn't want her going to the same school as their white children. Walking toward the school, Elizabeth felt her knees start to shake. Suddenly she wasn't sure she could make it. "It was," she said, "the longest block I ever walked in my whole life."

Finally she reached the entrance. She expected the soldiers to move aside and escort her into the building. Instead, they put their bayonets across the doorway and refused to let her enter. Only then did Elizabeth realize why they were there. Orval Faubus, the governor of Arkansas, had defied the court order. He had sent the soldiers to keep her out of the school.

Elizabeth became terrified. She didn't know what to do. Just then a member of the white mob cried, "Lynch her! Lynch her!" Elizabeth turned and searched the crowd, trying to find a friendly face. She spotted an old woman with kind-looking eyes. But when Elizabeth walked toward her, the old woman spat on her.

Unnerved, Elizabeth began to walk back toward the bus stop. She knew she wouldn't be safe until she could climb onto a bus and get out of the area. As she moved down the street, she kept her head up and her eyes focused straight ahead. She didn't want the crowd to know she was scared. By the time she reached the bus stop, the mob was in a frenzy. "Drag her over to this tree!" someone shouted. "Let's take care of the nigger!" screamed another.

At that point a white man stepped out of the crowd and went over to Elizabeth. He was a reporter for a Northern newspaper. Patting her on the shoulder, he whispered, "Don't let them see you cry." Elizabeth nodded. She knew how important it was to be strong. Although she felt petrified, she managed to appear calm until the bus arrived and carried her home. Only when she saw her mother did she begin to cry.

Elizabeth Eckford was not the only one who had to face the angry jeers of the crowd that morning. The eight other black students who showed up at Central High also had to confront the mob. One by one they approached the school, and one by one they were turned away by the guardsmen.

For the next two and a half weeks the black students stayed home. They had not given up, though. They were simply waiting for the tempers of the white racists to cool. By Monday, September 23, the soldiers had left Central High. On that day the nine teenagers tried again. They went to the school and entered the building. But whites in the community found out that they were there and soon began to gather outside. By mid-morning there were over a thousand of them. For a while they just milled restlessly about. Then they began to talk of violence. They threatened to break into the school and drag the black students out. City police arrived and tried to prevent trouble, but by noon the situation was almost out of control. Afraid of what might happen, the principal ordered the blacks to leave.

Two days later the president of the United States, Dwight Eisenhower, stepped in. Overruling Governor Faubus, he put the National Guard under federal control and ordered ten thousand guardsmen to protect the black students. He also sent in a thousand army paratroopers to walk the black students to their classes. Under tight military control then, the nine teenagers returned to Central High.

They were finally safe from the throngs of angry adults, but they still had to face the scorn and hatred of their fellow students. Each day white students found new ways to humiliate them. They spat on them, threw ink at them, and sent them nasty notes. They stole books from their lockers. They stuffed their jackets down toilets.

Minnejean Brown was singled out as a favorite target. Everywhere she went, she heard white students laughing at her and calling her names. She often went home bruised after being tripped or pushed down stairs. One day a white girl walked up behind her in the cafeteria and, before Minnejean could move, dumped a bowl of hot soup on her.

All year the torment continued. In November, the army paratroopers left, but the National Guard remained to keep the peace and protect the students. The blacks, who became known as the Little Rock Nine, remained lonely and isolated. Yet they never stopped going to Central High School. As one southern college professor said, "I cannot recall that there has ever been a more inspiring demonstration of courage by the children of any race, in any age."

At the end of the school year, the black students emerged from Central High exhausted but victorious. They had survived an entire year in the hostile environment of the school. They had opened the way for other blacks to begin attending white schools. They had even managed to make a few friends among the white students. When Ernest Green graduated that spring, fourteen whites asked to sign his yearbook. "I have admired your courage this year," one of them wrote, "and I'm glad you made it through all right." ∎

If you have been timed while reading this selection, enter your reading time below. Then turn to the Words per Minute table on page 155 and look up your reading speed (words per minute). Enter your reading speed on the graph on page 156.

READING TIME: Unit 13

———————— : ————————
Minutes   Seconds

How well did you read?

- *Answer the four types of questions that follow. The directions for each type of question tell you how to mark your answers.*

- *When you have finished all four exercises, check your work by using the answer key on page 151. For each right answer, put a check mark (✔) on the line beside the box. For each wrong answer, write the correct answer on the line.*

- *For scoring each exercise, follow the directions below the questions.*

A FINDING THE MAIN IDEA

Look at the three statements below. One expresses the main idea of the story you just read. A good main idea statement answers two questions: it tells *who* or *what* is the subject of the story, and it answers the understood question *does what?* or *is what?* Another statement is *too broad*, it is vague and doesn't tell much about the topic of the story. The third statement is *too narrow*, it tells about only one part of the story.

Match the statements with the three answer choices below by writing the letter of each answer in the box in front of the statement it goes with.

M—Main Idea   B—Too Broad   N—Too Narrow

_____ ☐ 1. Nine black teenagers in Little Rock, Arkansas, in 1957 courageously faced the hatred of the white community as they became the first blacks in the state to attend an all-white high school.

_____ ☐ 2. Orval Faubus, the governor of Arkansas in 1957, tried everything he could to keep from having to desegregate the public schools of Arkansas.

_____ ☐ 3. The first blacks to attend white public schools in Arkansas faced severe discrimination because of the great prejudice of the white community against blacks.

_____ Score 15 points for a correct *M* answer

_____ Score 5 points for each correct *B* or *N* answer

_____ TOTAL SCORE: Finding the Main Idea

B RECALLING FACTS

How well do you remember the facts in the story you just read? Put an *x* in the box in front of the correct answer to each of the multiple-choice questions below.

1. The bus dropped Elizabeth Eckford off
   - ___ ☐ a. in front of Central High.
   - ___ ☐ b. at the back door of Central High.
   - ___ ☐ c. one block from Central High.

2. The white man who patted Elizabeth's shoulder and said, "Don't let them see you cry" was
   - ___ ☐ a. the principal of Central High.
   - ___ ☐ b. a member of the Arkansas National Guard.
   - ___ ☐ c. a reporter for a Northern newspaper.

3. Dwight Eisenhower
   - ___ ☐ a. supported Governor Faubus's decision.
   - ___ ☐ b. ordered army paratroopers to walk the black students to classes.
   - ___ ☐ c. told the blacks to stay home until the tempers of the white people had cooled.

4. As Ernest Green prepared to graduate, fourteen whites
   - ___ ☐ a. asked to sign his yearbook.
   - ___ ☐ b. threatened to beat him.
   - ___ ☐ c. poured ink all over him.

5. By the end of the school year,
   - ___ ☐ a. all the black students had left Central High.
   - ___ ☐ b. the black students had made a few white friends.
   - ___ ☐ c. Governor Orval Faubus had left office.

Score 5 points for each correct answer

___ TOTAL SCORE: Recalling Facts

C MAKING INFERENCES

An inference is a judgment that is made or an idea that is arrived at based on facts or on information that is given. You make an inference when you understand something that is *not* stated directly, but that is *implied*, or suggested by the facts that are given.

Below are five statements that are judgments or ideas that have been arrived at from the facts of the story. Write the letter *C* in the box in front of each statement that is a correct inference. Write the letter *F* in front of each faulty inference.

C—Correct Inference   F—Faulty Inference

- ___ ☐ 1. The parents of the Little Rock Nine did not want their children to attend Central High.

- ___ ☐ 2. The desegregation of Central High School attracted national attention.

- ___ ☐ 3. Elizabeth Eckford knew she might run into trouble on her first day at the all-white high school.

- ___ ☐ 4. Arkansas was the only state that was against the desegregation of its schools.

- ___ ☐ 5. President Dwight Eisenhower did not have the legal authority to take control of the Arkansas National Guard.

Score 5 points for each correct answer

___ TOTAL SCORE: Making Inferences

D USING WORDS PRECISELY

Each of the numbered sentences below contains an underlined word or phrase from the story you have just read. Under the sentence are three definitions. One has the *same* meaning as the underlined word or phrase, one has *almost the same* meaning, and one has the *opposite* meaning. Match the definitions with the three answer choices by writing the letter that stands for each answer in the box in front of the definition it goes with.

S—Same   A—Almost the Same   O—Opposite

1. Orval Faubus, the governor of Arkansas, had <u>defied</u> the court order.

____ ☐ a. disobeyed

____ ☐ b. challenged

____ ☐ c. carried out

2. But they still had to face the <u>scorn</u> and hatred of their fellow students.

____ ☐ a. respect

____ ☐ b. disgust

____ ☐ c. contempt

3. Each day white students found new ways to <u>humiliate</u> them.

____ ☐ a. degrade

____ ☐ b. honor

____ ☐ c. embarrass

4. All year the <u>torment</u> continued.

____ ☐ a. punishment

____ ☐ b. persecution

____ ☐ c. kindness

5. The blacks, who became known as the Little Rock Nine, remained lonely and <u>isolated</u>.

____ ☐ a. cut off from others

____ ☐ b. in the middle of a group

____ ☐ c. withdrawn

____ Score 3 points for each correct S answer
____ Score 1 point for each correct A or O answer

____ TOTAL SCORE: Using Words Precisely

● *Enter the four total scores in the spaces below, and add them together to find your Critical Reading Score. Then record your Critical Reading Score on the graph on page 157.*

_____ Finding the Main Idea
_____ Recalling Facts
_____ Making Inferences
_____ Using Words Precisely

_____ CRITICAL READING SCORE: Unit 13

War does terrible things to a country and to its people. One of its saddest consequences is that children are left without parents, without homes, without anyone to care for them. When Richard Hughes went to Vietnam during the Vietnam War, his heart went out to the orphans who spent their days and nights in the dirty streets of the city of Saigon. But he did more than just feel pity for them. He stayed and took care of as many of them as he could.

Richard Hughes and the Dust of Life

Homeless children filled the streets. Dressed in rags, they wandered through back alleys and dug through garbage cans in search of food scraps. At night they curled up on street corners or in gutters to sleep. Some were sick and some had lost arms or legs in bomb explosions. To earn a little money, many of the young boys shined shoes, ran errands, or sold newspapers. Others learned to steal.

When Richard Hughes saw the street children, he was aghast. It was April 1968, and he had just arrived in Saigon, Vietnam. He was a twenty-four-year-old freelance reporter. He had come to Saigon to cover the Vietnam War. He wanted to keep the public informed as the United States and South Vietnam fought the communists of North Vietnam. But as he walked down the streets of the city, he realized he had a more significant job to do.

The orphaned Vietnamese street children were desperate. Their lives were so bleak that the Vietnamese called them "the dust of life." They needed food, medical care and a decent place to sleep. They needed someone to help them, and since no one else seemed interested, Richard decided he would be the one to do it.

Richard had traveled to Vietnam with only a single change of clothes and $400 in cash. But still he was determined to help the homeless children. He didn't have the resources to help them all, so he decided to concentrate on the younger boys. He spent most of his money, $325, to rent six rooms in a house on a busy side street. He then walked through the streets and invited orphaned boys to share the rooms with him. Soon eleven shoe-shine boys had moved in.

As more and more boys found their way to Richard's shelter, the rooms became crowded. Before long, over forty boys were living in the six rooms. Many had to sleep in the middle of the floor, but they didn't mind. It was better than sleeping in a tree or huddling all night in a doorway. Because Richard had very little money, he could not afford to buy meat or vegetables. Most meals consisted of French bread and peanut butter. But again, the boys didn't mind. In the street they had often gone days without any food at all.

Richard tried not to impose too many restrictions on the children. He let them come and go as they pleased. Many of them continued to work shining shoes or running errands. When one of them brought home a puppy from the street, the boys were allowed to keep it as a pet. There was only one thing Richard tried to

teach them: self-respect. In many ways, that was the hardest thing for them to learn. Many of the boys had seen their parents killed by soldiers. Some had been living in the streets since they were five or six years old. Some had been beaten by police who tried to steal what little money the boys had earned. Some had even become addicted to heroin.

As the boys settled into Richard's home, he tried to take care of them all. But it wasn't easy. Sometimes he was up all night comforting a sick child. Other times he had to break up fights between the boys. The most difficult thing of all, though, was his constant search for money.

When Richard's own money ran out, he began to ask for help from others. A few native Vietnamese doctors and dentists donated their services. So did a local barber and a lawyer. But Richard still needed money for food, rent and clothing. He started asking for contributions from private citizens in the United States. Only a few responded. Next he turned to large American businesses. Again he met with little success. One of the biggest oil companies in the world donated only a hundred dollars. Many other rich companies refused to give anything at all. For Richard, each day became a battle to raise funds to keep his shelter going. At one point he became so desperate for money that he sold the airline ticket he had been saving for his return home.

In spite of the enormous difficulties, though, Richard never gave up. In fact, he soon expanded his efforts. When he couldn't squeeze any more people into his six-room shelter, he opened two other homes in Saigon. He also traveled to the city of Da Nang and opened a home there. He found older boys to help run the shelters, and he took a part-time job to earn money to pay the bills. He also spent many hours setting up job-training programs for the boys. He managed to get many of them enrolled in woodworking or motor repair classes.

In 1970, Richard started thinking of returning to the United States. He felt that the older boys were capable of taking over full responsibility for running the homes. For two years Richard thought about the possibility of leaving. But he could never bring himself to do it. The same questions kept running through his head. "What will happen when I leave? How will the children look at me when I go? What will I say to them as I leave?" Finally he realized that he could not leave. He vowed not to go until his children had some hope for a brighter future. "If I left early," he said, "the faces of those kids would haunt me forever."

So Richard Hughes stayed in Vietnam. In April of 1975, the communists of the north took over South Vietnam. The United States military pulled out, and civilians fled. But Richard remained. He stayed for another year and a half, helping to rebuild the lives of the street children. With the war over, many were able to get work on farms or in shops. Some even found family members they had thought were dead. As the boys were accepted back into society, Richard began to close his shelters. Finally, in August of 1976, he left Vietnam. He was the last American to leave the country.

Looking back on his eight years in Vietnam, Richard Hughes was pleased with his work. He had operated a total of seven shelters. More than fifteen hundred street children had found their way to his doorstep. He knew he had not saved all the homeless children in Vietnam. Thousands had remained in the streets, untouched by his efforts. Nonetheless, he had done what no one else had bothered to do. He had given love, protection and hope to children who had been labeled "the dust of life." ∎

If you have been timed while reading this selection, enter your reading time below. Then turn to the Words per Minute table on page 155 and look up your reading speed (words per minute). Enter your reading speed on the graph on page 156.

READING TIME: Unit 14

——————— : ———————
Minutes   *Seconds*

How well did you read?

- *Answer the four types of questions that follow. The directions for each type of question tell you how to mark your answers.*

- *When you have finished all four exercises, check your work by using the answer key on page 151. For each right answer, put a check mark (✔) on the line beside the box. For each wrong answer, write the correct answer on the line.*

- *For scoring each exercise, follow the directions below the questions.*

A FINDING THE MAIN IDEA

Look at the three statements below. One expresses the main idea of the story you just read. A good main idea statement answers two questions: it tells *who* or *what* is the subject of the story, and it answers the understood question *does what?* or *is what?* Another statement is *too broad,* it is vague and doesn't tell much about the topic of the story. The third statement is *too narrow,* it tells about only one part of the story.

Match the statements with the three answer choices below by writing the letter of each answer in the box in front of the statement it goes with.

M—Main Idea   **B—Too Broad**   **N—Too Narrow**

_____ ☐ 1. Richard Hughes, a freelance newspaper reporter, lived in Vietnam for eight years.

_____ ☐ 2. Richard Hughes was a kind and generous person who did a great deal of good for the people of Vietnam.

_____ ☐ 3. Richard Hughes gave help and hope to homeless Vietnamese children by opening shelters for them.

_____ Score 15 points for a correct *M* answer

_____ Score 5 points for each correct *B* or *N* answer

_____ TOTAL SCORE: Finding the Main Idea

B RECALLING FACTS

How well do you remember the facts in the story you just read? Put an *x* in the box in front of the correct answer to each of the multiple-choice questions below.

1. Richard Hughes went to Vietnam to
   - ☐ a. open shelters for homeless children.
   - ☐ b. raise money for orphans.
   - ☐ c. report on the war that was being fought there.

2. Most of the meals Richard served to the children consisted of
   - ☐ a. meat.
   - ☐ b. fruits and vegetables.
   - ☐ c. bread and peanut butter.

3. At one point Richard sold his airline ticket because
   - ☐ a. he needed money to pay bills.
   - ☐ b. he decided he wanted to stay in Vietnam.
   - ☐ c. the airport in Saigon was taken over by communists.

4. For Richard, the hardest part of running his shelter was
   - ☐ a. keeping the boys from fighting.
   - ☐ b. teaching the boys woodworking and motor repair.
   - ☐ c. finding money to keep the shelter going.

5. Richard Hughes opened most of his shelters in
   - ☐ a. Da Nang.
   - ☐ b. Saigon.
   - ☐ c. North Vietnam.

Score 5 points for each correct answer

_____ TOTAL SCORE: Recalling Facts

C MAKING INFERENCES

An inference is a judgment that is made or an idea that is arrived at based on facts or on information that is given. You make an inference when you understand something that is *not* stated directly, but that is *implied*, or suggested by the facts that are given.

Below are five statements that are judgments or ideas that have been arrived at from the facts of the story. Write the letter *C* in the box in front of each statement that is a correct inference. Write the letter *F* in front of each faulty inference.

C—Correct Inference   F—Faulty Inference

- ☐ 1. The children whom Richard Hughes helped were grateful to him.

- ☐ 2. The street children whom Richard could not help had to remain forever outside Vietnamese society.

- ☐ 3. It was hard for Richard to convince people outside Vietnam of the desperate needs of the street children.

- ☐ 4. The street children were looked upon as criminals by the Vietnamese people.

- ☐ 5. Richard Hughes was the only person in Vietnam who cared about the street children.

Score 5 points for each correct answer

_____ TOTAL SCORE: Making Inferences

D USING WORDS PRECISELY

Each of the numbered sentences below contains an underlined word or phrase from the story you have just read. Under the sentence are three definitions. One has the *same* meaning as the underlined word or phrase, one has *almost the same* meaning, and one has the *opposite* meaning. Match the definitions with the three answer choices by writing the letter that stands for each answer in the box in front of the definition it goes with.

S—Same   A—Almost the Same   O—Opposite

1. When Richard Hughes saw the street children, he was underline{aghast}.

____ ☐ a. shocked

____ ☐ b. unmoved

____ ☐ c. surprised

2. But as he walked down the streets of the city, he realized he had a more underline{significant} job to do.

____ ☐ a. special

____ ☐ b. important

____ ☐ c. meaningless

3. Their lives were so underline{bleak} that the Vietnamese called them "the dust of life."

____ ☐ a. promising

____ ☐ b. dismal

____ ☐ c. sad

4. Richard tried not to underline{impose} too many restrictions on the children.

____ ☐ a. demand

____ ☐ b. withdraw

____ ☐ c. place

5. In fact, he soon underline{expanded} his efforts. When he couldn't squeeze any more people into the six-room shelter, he opened two other homes in Saigon.

____ ☐ a. broadened

____ ☐ b. inflated

____ ☐ c. reduced

____ Score 3 points for each correct *S* answer
____ Score 1 point for each correct *A* or *O* answer

____ TOTAL SCORE: Using Words Precisely

● *Enter the four total scores in the spaces below, and add them together to find your Critical Reading Score. Then record your Critical Reading Score on the graph on page 157.*

_____ Finding the Main Idea
_____ Recalling Facts
_____ Making Inferences
_____ Using Words Precisely

_____ CRITICAL READING SCORE: Unit 14

GROUP THREE

Roberto Clemente was a great baseball player—one of the best. But his interests and his efforts stretched far beyond the baseball diamond. He wanted to contribute something to the world—to give something back to the Latin American countries that cheered him as their greatest sports hero. He found the opportunity to give a great deal.

Roberto Clemente: A Duty to Others

For more than a decade he had been one of the greatest baseball players of all time. He could hit, run and throw with power and grace. And on September 30, 1972, he was one step away from baseball immortality. Roberto Clemente of Puerto Rico and the Pittsburgh Pirates was just one hit shy of three thousand hits. Only ten other players in the 103-year history of the game had collected that many hits.

At Three Rivers Stadium in Pittsburgh, over thirteen thousand Pirate fans were pulling for Roberto. Throughout Latin America, hundreds of thousands more sat glued to their radios, waiting for the historic hit. When Roberto stepped up to the plate, the fans stood and cheered wildly. On the mound for the New York Mets was a young pitcher named Jon Matlack. Roberto dug in at the plate, cocked his bat high over his head, and glared at Matlack. The pitcher fired a fastball and the Pirate star swung hard, drilling the ball on a line to deep left-center field for a double. The fans roared with delight. What the fans couldn't know, however, was that that hit was to be Roberto's last.

When the baseball season ended a few days later, Roberto returned to his home in Puerto Rico. At that point, he was the greatest sports hero in all of Latin America. But he was not admirable only when he was on the playing field. Off the field, too, Roberto Clemente was a man of conviction and strength. Baseball had won him fame and money, but he hadn't forgotten that most people in Latin America were poor. He felt he had a duty to help those who hadn't been as lucky as he had.

One way he tried to help was by volunteering to manage an amateur Puerto Rican baseball team. In November, the team traveled to Nicaragua to play in a tournament. While Roberto was in Managua, the capital city of Nicaragua, he met a fourteen-year-old orphan named Julio. Julio had lost both his legs in an accident, but had no money for a wheelchair or artificial legs. Without fanfare, Roberto arranged to get Julio a pair of artificial legs. On December 6, when the baseball tournament was over, Roberto flew back to Puerto Rico to be with his family.

Less than three weeks later, a devastating event took place. On the morning of December 23, a huge earthquake leveled Managua. It uprooted trees, toppled power lines, and flattened buildings. Worse still, it killed over six thousand people and left another twenty thousand injured. Although it was Christmastime and the Clementes had planned holiday celebrations, Roberto did not hesitate. He quickly organized the Puerto Rican Relief Fund for Nicaragua.

Just as he gave everything he had when playing baseball, Roberto threw himself into the relief effort with every ounce of his energy. On television and radio, he urged people to donate whatever they could to help the victims of the earthquake. He collected food, medicine and clothing. He forgot all about eating and sleeping. He even had a radiotelephone installed at his home so that he could keep in touch with the relief work at Managua Airport. There would be no Christmas-as-usual for Roberto and his family.

The biggest problem Roberto faced was how to get the supplies to Nicaragua. He arranged to have the *San Expedito*, a cargo ship, transport most of the supplies. But the ship was slow. For speed, planes were needed. Roberto organized three special flights to Managua. They carried the vital supplies that were needed immediately.

To most people, it seemed that Roberto had done all he could. But on the morning of December 31, there was an urgent request from the rescue workers in Managua. They needed more medical supplies, a water pump, and an X-ray machine. Roberto decided to take the things to Managua himself. Many of his friends were distressed. It was New Year's Eve, and they thought he should stay with his family. After all, they argued, he had already missed Christmas. They pleaded with him to spend the holiday at home and go to Managua later. But Roberto insisted on making the flight. "I have to go," he said. "Those people are my friends. The least I can do is to be with them tonight. And I need to find Julio. I need to see if he is all right. Besides, there are babies dying over there; they need these supplies."

The plane Roberto rented was a twenty-year-old DC-7. It had been in two minor accidents and it had a history of mechanical failures. It had not been flown in over four months. But it was the only plane available on such short notice. Because Roberto knew it was critical to get the supplies to Managua, he decided to take the chance that the plane was safe.

Two colleagues from the relief effort volunteered to go along. The three men and the pilot and copilot were ready to go by four o'clock that afternoon. But the plane still needed some mechanical work. It was 5 P.M. before the work was completed. Roberto kissed his wife goodbye and climbed into the plane. The rickety DC-7 started down the runway and stopped. More mechanical adjustments had to be made. Worried, Roberto got out of the plane to talk to the mechanic. "One more delay," he said, "and I won't go tonight. I'll wait until tomorrow."

Finally, a little after 9 P.M., the mechanic announced that the plane was ready. Once again it sped down the runway. At exactly 9:22 P.M., the plane lifted off and banked to the left. But suddenly it disappeared from the radar screen in the control tower. Moments later, the plane carrying Roberto Clemente and the other four men crashed into the Atlantic Ocean. It hit the water about a mile offshore, floated for a few seconds, then sank. Roberto's body was never recovered.

Until his tragic death, many people had not been aware of Roberto's selfless dedication to the people of Latin America. Within a few days, however, word of his actions had spread around the world. People in Latin America and the United States held silent marches to honor him. The following year, he was overwhelmingly elected to baseball's Hall of Fame. He was the first Latin American to be so honored. Also, it was the only time in the history of baseball that the five-year waiting period for election to the Hall of Fame was waived. But Roberto Clemente was more than a hero to baseball fans. He was a hero to everyone. ■

If you have been timed while reading this selection, enter your reading time below. Then turn to the Words per Minute table on page 155 and look up your reading speed (words per minute). Enter your reading speed on the graph on page 156.

READING TIME: Unit 15

_____ : _____
Minutes   Seconds

How well did you read?

- *Answer the four types of questions that follow. The directions for each type of question tell you how to mark your answers.*

- *When you have finished all four exercises, check your work by using the answer key on page 152. For each right answer, put a check mark (✔) on the line beside the box. For each wrong answer, write the correct answer on the line.*

- *For scoring each exercise, follow the directions below the questions.*

A FINDING THE MAIN IDEA

Look at the three statements below. One expresses the main idea of the story you just read. A good main idea statement answers two questions: it tells *who* or *what* is the subject of the story, and it answers the understood question *does what?* or *is what?* Another statement is *too broad*, it is vague and doesn't tell much about the topic of the story. The third statement is *too narrow*, it tells about only one part of the story.

Match the statements with the three answer choices below by writing the letter of each answer in the box in front of the statement it goes with.

M—Main Idea   **B—Too Broad**   **N—Too Narrow**

_____ ☐ 1. Roberto Clemente was the first Latin American baseball player to be elected to the Hall of Fame.

_____ ☐ 2. Roberto Clemente, like many well-known sports figures, contributed much to his community.

_____ ☐ 3. Roberto Clemente was not only a great baseball player, but a great human being as well.

_____ Score 15 points for a correct *M* answer

_____ Score 5 points for each correct *B* or *N* answer

_____ TOTAL SCORE: Finding the Main Idea

B RECALLING FACTS

How well do you remember the facts in the story you just read? Put an *x* in the box in front of the correct answer to each of the multiple-choice questions below.

1. Roberto Clemente's three thousandth hit was a
   - ____ ☐ a. single.
   - ____ ☐ b. double.
   - ____ ☐ c. triple.

2. The city hit by the earthquake was
   - ____ ☐ a. Pittsburgh.
   - ____ ☐ b. San Juan.
   - ____ ☐ c. Managua.

3. The first time Roberto went to Managua in 1972, he was
   - ____ ☐ a. the head of a relief mission.
   - ____ ☐ b. the manager of a baseball team.
   - ____ ☐ c. on tour with the Pittsburgh Pirates.

4. Roberto had a radiotelephone installed in his home so that he could keep in touch with the
   - ____ ☐ a. Managua Airport.
   - ____ ☐ b. Pittsburgh Pirates.
   - ____ ☐ c. *San Expedito.*

5. Roberto Clemente died on
   - ____ ☐ a. Christmas Day.
   - ____ ☐ b. New Year's Day.
   - ____ ☐ c. New Year's Eve.

Score 5 points for each correct answer

____ TOTAL SCORE: Recalling Facts

C MAKING INFERENCES

An inference is a judgment that is made or an idea that is arrived at based on facts or on information that is given. You make an inference when you understand something that is *not* stated directly, but that is *implied*, or suggested by the facts that are given.

Below are five statements that are judgments or ideas that have been arrived at from the facts of the story. Write the letter *C* in the box in front of each statement that is a correct inference. Write the letter *F* in front of each faulty inference.

C—Correct Inference   F—Faulty Inference

- ____ ☐ 1. If Roberto Clemente had not died, he would have gone on to be the greatest baseball player of all time.

- ____ ☐ 2. If Roberto had not met Julio in Nicaragua, he would probably not have headed the relief fund.

- ____ ☐ 3. Roberto Clemente's fame as a baseball player helped him get aid for the people of Managua.

- ____ ☐ 4. If Roberto had lived, he would have given up baseball and dedicated the rest of his life to helping the poor of Latin America.

- ____ ☐ 5. Roberto Clemente cared more for the people of Managua than he did for his own family.

Score 5 points for each correct answer

____ TOTAL SCORE: Making Inferences

D USING WORDS PRECISELY

Each of the numbered sentences below contains an underlined word or phrase from the story you have just read. Under the sentence are three definitions. One has the *same* meaning as the underlined word or phrase, one has *almost the same* meaning, and one has the *opposite* meaning. Match the definitions with the three answer choices by writing the letter that stands for each answer in the box in front of the definition it goes with.

S—Same   A—Almost the Same   O—Opposite

1. But he was not <u>admirable</u> only when he was on the playing field.

  ____ ☐ a. well-liked

  ____ ☐ b. worthless

  ____ ☐ c. praiseworthy

2. They carried the <u>vital</u> supplies that were needed immediately.

  ____ ☐ a. of the greatest importance

  ____ ☐ b. highly useful

  ____ ☐ c. unimportant

3. Many of his friends were <u>distressed</u>.

  ____ ☐ a. unhappy

  ____ ☐ b. upset

  ____ ☐ c. relieved

4. The <u>rickety</u> DC-7 started down the runway and stopped.

  ____ ☐ a. run-down

  ____ ☐ b. weak

  ____ ☐ c. sturdy

5. It was the only time in the history of baseball that the five-year waiting period for election to the Hall of Fame was <u>waived</u>.

  ____ ☐ a. enforced

  ____ ☐ b. set aside

  ____ ☐ c. questioned

  ____ Score 3 points for each correct *S* answer
  ____ Score 1 point for each correct *A* or *O* answer

  ____ TOTAL SCORE: Using Words Precisely

● *Enter the four total scores in the spaces below, and add them together to find your Critical Reading Score. Then record your Critical Reading Score on the graph on page 157.*

_____ Finding the Main Idea
_____ Recalling Facts
_____ Making Inferences
_____ Using Words Precisely
_____ CRITICAL READING SCORE: Unit 15

Frank Serpico: An Honest Cop

Police officer Frank Serpico lay in the Brooklyn Jewish Hospital in critical condition. Four days earlier, on February 3, 1971, he had been shot in the head while trying to arrest a heroin dealer. Luckily the bullet had not reached Serpico's brain. But it had torn through his facial muscles, crashed through his left sinus and hit his jawbone. His face was swollen to twice its normal size, and a bloody fluid oozed from his ear. The doctors were not yet sure if he would live.

As he lay conscious but heavily sedated, a nurse brought him an envelope. Inside was a greeting card bearing the printed message "Recuperate Quickly." But the person who sent the card had crossed out the word *Recuperate* and had written in the word *Die*.

Although the card was not signed, Serpico was sure it was from a fellow cop. Only a member of the New York Police Department would have sent such a vicious message. Serpico knew that most of the men and women in the department hated him, or at least mistrusted him. He had broken the number one rule of the force. He had exposed the corruption of his fellow officers. In their view, Frank Serpico had squealed.

When Serpico became a police officer in early 1960, he just wanted to be a good,
honest cop. He soon learned that that wasn't so easy. Almost immediately, he discovered that most of the officers on the force did not share his lofty vision of police work. To Serpico, being a cop meant upholding the law, protecting honest citizens from outlaws, and setting a good example for society. To most of his coworkers in the 81st Precinct, however, being a cop simply meant having a good, steady job with the opportunity to make lots of money.

In his early days on the force, Serpico was amazed by what he saw. He found that many cops beat their suspects. Others slept on the job or demanded free meals from local restaurants in return for special favors. Worst of all, most of the officers in the precinct accepted bribes. At first the bribes that Serpico learned about were small—thirty dollars or so for letting someone get away with a traffic violation. But when Serpico moved up into the plain-clothes division, he saw that the problem of graft was a lot bigger than that.

While working as an undercover cop, Serpico discovered that virtually all plainclothes officers were corrupt. Almost all of them accepted many thousands of dollars in bribes each year. The bribes came from people who were operating illegal gambling rackets. In return for the
money, cops allowed the gamblers to continue their illegal activities. Those few officers who weren't taking money simply looked the other way while their partners got richer and richer.

At first Frank just looked the other way too. Time after time, he refused to take the payoffs that were offered to him. Gradually, however, he began to feel that he needed to do something more. He couldn't continue to stand by and watch while hundreds of dishonest police officers worked out illegal deals with gamblers. Still, he wasn't sure what to do. The more he thought about it, the more convinced he became that many of his superior officers were also accepting bribes.

Serpico pondered the situation for months. Then, in July of 1966, something happened that forced him into action. A uniformed cop handed him an envelope, telling him it was from the ringleader of a gambling circle in the district. When Serpico opened the envelope, he found that it contained three hundred dollars in small bills. It was then that he knew he could not ignore the problem any longer. He had to report the incident to the authorities. But whom could he trust? How could he know which of his superior officers were honest and which weren't? How could he make sure that his charges would lead to an investigation and not to a cover-up?

There were no clear answers to any of those questions, but Serpico knew he had to tell someone what was going on. He began to contact high-ranking police officers outside his precinct. He talked to one after another, but no one seemed willing to do anything. Some were too scared, some were too lazy, and some were probably guilty of illegal activities themselves. In any event, Frank Serpico kept trying. He went to division captains, to the deputy chief inspector, to the commissioner of investigation, and to one of the mayor's closest advisors in city hall. He even sent messages to the police commissioner's first deputy, who was in charge of all police matters. Still nothing happened.

Meanwhile, the cops on the force began to get suspicious of Serpico. They resented the fact that he didn't take bribes. They began to worry that he was going to squeal on them. Soon, only a few of the plainclothes officers in his division would talk to him.

Finally, after fighting with top officials for a year and a half, Serpico got some results. A small investigation was made into his allegations of graft and corruption. But because the investigation was handled poorly, it turned up only enough

In 1971, Frank Serpico testified in front of a commission organized to look into charges of widespread corruption in the New York City Police Department. He accused fellow officers and high-ranking law enforcement officials of accepting bribes in return for turning their backs on known illegal activities. For years Serpico's honesty had made him unpopular with other members of the force. But his public accusations of crime in the police department won him many more enemies.

evidence to arrest eight plainclothes cops. No higher-ranking officers were charged, and nothing was done to restructure the system.

Still, word spread quickly through the entire police department that Serpico had squealed. After that, almost no one on the force wanted anything to do with him. No one wanted to be his partner for daily assignments. Conversations stopped whenever he entered a room. One day a fellow cop even pulled a switchblade on him while a dozen other officers stood by and watched.

During that period, Serpico almost gave up. He had risked his career and endangered his own life in an effort to improve the system. Yet it appeared that little was going to change. He had hoped that the department could clean itself up, but clearly that was not the case. So, in desperation, Serpico decided to make his allegations public. Early in 1970, he took his story to the *New York Times*.

When people read Serpico's story in the newspaper, they were outraged. The public demanded a full-scale investigation. As a result, a special commission was created to look into the widespread problem of crime within the police force. The commission conducted the most thorough probe in the history of the New York Police Department. As a result, stricter rules were developed to help prevent police corruption in the future. Many of the top officials who had refused to cooperate with Serpico were eventually forced to resign.

While all that was happening, Frank Serpico went on trying to be a good cop. He was transferred to the narcotics division in Brooklyn South, and he worked hard to combat the drug trade that flourished there. But again he met with resistance and distrust from his fellow officers. Again he encountered cops who were taking bribes from local criminals. Although in Brooklyn South he worked with three partners, he didn't really trust any of them. In fact, on the night he was shot in the head, he felt that none of his partners rushed to help him.

It took Serpico months to recover from the bullet wound he suffered that night. Though he remained deaf in his left ear and unable to walk without a cane, his recovery was remarkable. As he regained his strength, however, he realized that his life was a shambles. He had sacrificed his future for the sake of his ideals. He had never stopped trying to be a good cop, but the effort had cost him dearly. After thinking it over, Frank Serpico decided not to return to the New York Police Department. Instead, he left the country to try to sort out his shattered life.

Serpico had discovered that fighting for right and justice can be difficult and lonely. He had suffered greatly for the sake of his values. But through his perseverance he had righted some wrongs. He had made a difference. ■

If you have been timed while reading this selection, enter your reading time below. Then turn to the Words per Minute table on page 155 and look up your reading speed (words per minute). Enter your reading speed on the graph on page 156.

┌─────────────────────────────────┐
│ READING TIME: Unit 16   │
│   │
│ _____ : _____   │
│ *Minutes*   *Seconds*   │
└─────────────────────────────────┘

How well did you read?

- *Answer the four types of questions that follow. The directions for each type of question tell you how to mark your answers.*

- *When you have finished all four exercises, check your work by using the answer key on page 152. For each right answer, put a check mark (✔) on the line beside the box. For each wrong answer, write the correct answer on the line.*

- *For scoring each exercise, follow the directions below the questions.*

A FINDING THE MAIN IDEA

Look at the three statements below. One expresses the main idea of the story you just read. A good main idea statement answers two questions: it tells *who* or *what* is the subject of the story, and it answers the understood question *does what?* or *is what?* Another statement is *too broad*, it is vague and doesn't tell much about the topic of the story. The third statement is *too narrow*, it tells about only one part of the story.

Match the statements with the three answer choices below by writing the letter of each answer in the box in front of the statement it goes with.

M—Main Idea   B—Too Broad   N—Too Narrow

_____ ☐ 1. Frank Serpico was a man who had high ideals and paid dearly for trying to uphold them.

_____ ☐ 2. Frank Serpico forced New York City public officials to form a commission to investigate corruption in the police department.

_____ ☐ 3. Frank Serpico was an extremely honest cop who fought corruption in the New York Police Department and suffered for his efforts.

_____ Score 15 points for a correct *M* answer
_____ Score 5 points for each correct *B* or *N* answer

_____ TOTAL SCORE: Finding the Main Idea

B RECALLING FACTS

How well do you remember the facts in the story you just read? Put an *x* in the box in front of the correct answer to each of the multiple-choice questions below.

1. To Frank Serpico, being a cop meant
   - ☐ a. having a good, steady job.
   - ☐ b. protecting honest citizens against criminals.
   - ☐ c. the chance to become a famous hero.

2. When Serpico first became aware of the corruption on the police force, he
   - ☐ a. tried to ignore it.
   - ☐ b. asked to be transferred to a new division.
   - ☐ c. reported his findings to his division captain.

3. Serpico decided to go to higher authorities when
   - ☐ a. a cop handed him an envelope containing three hundred dollars.
   - ☐ b. a fellow officer pulled a switchblade on him.
   - ☐ c. he found police officers accepting free meals from restaurants in return for favors.

4. As a result of the *New York Times* article,
   - ☐ a. eight plainclothes cops were arrested.
   - ☐ b. a special commission was formed to look into the problem of corruption on the police force.
   - ☐ c. Serpico decided to retire from the police force.

5. When Serpico was shot he was a member of
   - ☐ a. the 81st Precinct.
   - ☐ b. the Department of Investigation.
   - ☐ c. the Brooklyn South narcotics division.

Score 5 points for each correct answer

_____ TOTAL SCORE: Recalling Facts

C MAKING INFERENCES

An inference is a judgment that is made or an idea that is arrived at based on facts or on information that is given. You make an inference when you understand something that is *not* stated directly, but that is *implied*, or suggested by the facts that are given.

Below are five statements that are judgments or ideas that have been arrived at from the facts of the story. Write the letter *C* in the box in front of each statement that is a correct inference. Write the letter *F* in front of each faulty inference.

C—Correct Inference   F—Faulty Inference

1. ☐ Serpico ignored the small bribes he witnessed at first because he hoped it was not a serious problem.

2. ☐ Serpico thought it was all right for cops to take bribes as long as the bribes were only for traffic violations.

3. ☐ Police departments everywhere have serious problems with corruption.

4. ☐ Frank Serpico was the only good cop on the New York Police force.

5. ☐ If Serpico had not gone to the *New York Times*, a full-scale investigation would not have been conducted.

Score 5 points for each correct answer

_____ TOTAL SCORE: Making Inferences

D USING WORDS PRECISELY

Each of the numbered sentences below contains an underlined word or phrase from the story you have just read. Under the sentence are three definitions. One has the *same* meaning as the underlined word or phrase, one has *almost the same* meaning, and one has the *opposite* meaning. Match the definitions with the three answer choices by writing the letter that stands for each answer in the box in front of the definition it goes with.

S—Same   A—Almost the Same   O—Opposite

1. Inside was a greeting card bearing the printed message, "Recuperate Quickly."

____ ☐ a. get well

____ ☐ b. improve

____ ☐ c. become sicker

2. Serpico pondered the situation for months.

____ ☐ a. wondered about

____ ☐ b. ignored

____ ☐ c. thought carefully about

3. A small investigation was made into his allegations of graft and corruption.

____ ☐ a. denials

____ ☐ b. claims

____ ☐ c. beliefs

4. He was transferred to the narcotics division in Brooklyn South, and he worked hard to combat the drug trade that flourished there.

____ ☐ a. was dying out

____ ☐ b. thrived

____ ☐ c. was successful

5. As he regained his strength, however, he realized that his life was a shambles.

____ ☐ a. well-ordered place

____ ☐ b. mess

____ ☐ c. problem

____ Score 3 points for each correct S answer
____ Score 1 point for each correct A or O answer

____ TOTAL SCORE: Using Words Precisely

● *Enter the four total scores in the spaces below, and add them together to find your Critical Reading Score. Then record your Critical Reading Score on the graph on page 157.*

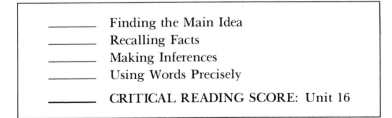

_____ Finding the Main Idea
_____ Recalling Facts
_____ Making Inferences
_____ Using Words Precisely

_____ CRITICAL READING SCORE: Unit 16

She was willing to do almost anything to get a story. Sometimes her determination to get at the truth placed her in great danger. But Nellie Bly was an eager and dedicated reporter, and it was that strong drive and hard work that allowed her to break into the man's world of journalism in the late 1800s. She went on to become one of the most respected newspaper reporters of her day.

Nellie Bly: Exposing the Truth

It was the most dangerous assignment Nellie Bly was ever offered. In 1888, Joseph Pulitzer, owner of the famous newspaper *The World*, asked her to write an article for his paper. He wanted her to investigate rumors of cruelty and neglect in the New York City insane asylum on Blackwells Island. The hospital was designed to care for insane people who had no money for private treatment. There had recently been many stories of patient abuse at the hospital. But because doctors would not let reporters talk to the patients, no one knew if the stories were accurate. The only way for Nellie to learn the truth was to become a patient herself. That meant she had to pretend she was crazy.

Nellie was willing to do that because she knew it might help those who were mentally ill. But she was worried about one thing. If she succeeded in getting into the hospital, how would she ever get out? Joseph Pulitzer told her not to worry; he promised he would take care of that. But when Nellie asked him what he intended to do, he admitted that he didn't know. He told her she would just have to trust him. Although Nellie feared that she might end up trapped behind the walls of the insane asylum forever, she agreed to go ahead with the assignment. It was her only chance to uncover the truth.

After agreeing to write the article, she went to a boardinghouse and rented a room. As soon as she moved in, she began to roll her eyes and act strangely. She claimed she could not remember her own name, and she accused everyone in the boardinghouse of being crazy. Within a few hours she had frightened the landlady and all the other boarders. The landlady called the police, who took Nellie to a nearby hospital for an examination. Nellie was not sure she could fool trained professionals into thinking she was insane, but to her surprise, the doctors asked her only a few very basic questions. Then they concluded that she was, indeed, hopelessly insane.

Because it appeared that Nellie didn't have any money, the doctors put her on a boat and shipped her off to the insane asylum on Blackwells Island. When the boat landed and she stepped ashore, a guard grabbed her. Pretending to be confused, she asked where she was. "This is a place for insane people," the guard snarled, "and you'll never leave it." Although Nellie believed that Joseph Pulitzer would do his best to get her released, those words still sent a shiver down her spine.

After being admitted to the hospital, Nellie immediately dropped her disguise and started acting perfectly normal. She wanted to see how the staff would react when they realized one of their patients was not sick. To her amazement, no one noticed. When she approached a doctor to talk to him, he ignored her. The same thing happened when she tried to start a conversation with a nurse. It didn't seem to matter what Nellie said or did—everyone just assumed that her actions were those of a crazy person.

Nellie soon learned that the staff did not pay much attention to any of the patients. She had expected medical care at the hospital to be minimal, but she was not prepared for the kind of heartless treatment that she saw all around her. Doctors routinely ignored the requests and complaints of the patients. Nurses beat those who were uncooperative. Sometimes staff members even banged patients' heads against the wall for no reason at all.

Nellie was equally stunned by the filthy living conditions that prevailed throughout the hospital. Once a week nurses forced her and the other female patients to take baths in ice-cold water. In the evenings guards locked them up in tiny, unheated rooms. The staff made them sleep in thin little slips and would not give them any blankets. In the daytime nurses tied all the patients together with ropes and led them outside like cattle for "outdoor exercise." Meals consisted of nothing more than bread, tea and a few shriveled prunes. When Nellie tried to eat the bread, she found that it was old and stale. One morning she even found a spider in it.

After a couple of days in that inhumane environment, Nellie was ready to get out. When she tried to explain to a doctor that she was not sick, however, he simply laughed and walked away. There was nothing she could do but wait and hope that Joseph Pulitzer would keep his promise to get her released. Finally, after ten days, Pulitzer came through. He sent a lawyer to Blackwells Island to arrange for Nellie's release. In order to get her out, the lawyer said that some of Nellie's friends had agreed to pay for private treatment.

As soon as Nellie was freed, she began to work on her story. When she finished, Pulitzer ran it on the front page of *The World*. The story instantly created a scandal, stirring the public's concern for the mentally ill. Health inspectors made a complete tour of the asylum and ordered the staff to improve conditions. Doctors at other hospitals began to conduct more careful examinations before declaring a person insane, and New York City increased its budget for care of the mentally ill by one million dollars.

Nellie was delighted that her newspaper article helped to change the city's attitude toward the mentally ill. She was also happy that Joseph Pulitzer liked her work. He was so impressed, in fact, that he offered her a permanent job as a reporter for *The World*. That made her the first female reporter on Pulitzer's entire staff.

Nellie went on to write many other compelling newspaper articles. Among them were articles that exposed the poor treatment of factory workers and the struggles of the new labor unions. As one of the first women in her field, she also led the way for other female journalists. When she died in 1922, New York newspapers mourned the death of "the best reporter in America." ■

If you have been timed while reading this selection, enter your reading time below. Then turn to the Words per Minute table on page 155 and look up your reading speed (words per minute). Enter your reading speed on the graph on page 156.

READING TIME: Unit 17
_____ : _____
Minutes   *Seconds*

How well did you read?

- *Answer the four types of questions that follow. The directions for each type of question tell you how to mark your answers.*

- *When you have finished all four exercises, check your work by using the answer key on page 152. For each right answer, put a check mark (✔) on the line beside the box. For each wrong answer, write the correct answer on the line.*

- *For scoring each exercise, follow the directions below the questions.*

A FINDING THE MAIN IDEA

Look at the three statements below. One expresses the main idea of the story you just read. A good main idea statement answers two questions: it tells *who* or *what* is the subject of the story, and it answers the understood question *does what?* or *is what?* Another statement is *too broad*, it is vague and doesn't tell much about the topic of the story. The third statement is *too narrow*, it tells about only one part of the story.

Match the statements with the three answer choices below by writing the letter of each answer in the box in front of the statement it goes with.

M—Main Idea   B—Too Broad   N—Too Narrow

_____ ☐ 1. Nellie Bly posed as a mentally ill person to get into the insane asylum on Blackwells Island.

_____ ☐ 2. Nellie Bly uncovered and exposed the horrors on Blackwells Island, and went on to become a great newspaper reporter.

_____ ☐ 3. Nellie Bly was one of the greatest newspaper reporters of the late nineteenth and early twentieth centuries.

_____ Score 15 points for a correct *M* answer

_____ Score 5 points for each correct *B* or *N* answer

_____ TOTAL SCORE: Finding the Main Idea

B RECALLING FACTS

How well do you remember the facts in the story you just read?
Put an *x* in the box in front of the correct answer to each of the multiple-choice questions below.

1. The insane asylum on Blackwells Island was intended for
   - ____ ☐ a. poor people who were physically ill.
   - ____ ☐ b. poor people who were mentally ill.
   - ____ ☐ c. old people who had no money.

2. When Nellie stopped acting crazy, the doctors and nurses
   - ____ ☐ a. became suspicious.
   - ____ ☐ b. didn't notice.
   - ____ ☐ c. put spiders in her food to frighten her.

3. When Nellie tried to talk to the doctors and nurses in the hospital, they
   - ____ ☐ a. beat her.
   - ____ ☐ b. ignored her.
   - ____ ☐ c. locked her in an unheated room.

4. Nellie stayed in the insane asylum
   - ____ ☐ a. ten days.
   - ____ ☐ b. five days.
   - ____ ☐ c. two days.

5. As a result of Nellie's article, New York City
   - ____ ☐ a. closed the hospital on Blackwells Island.
   - ____ ☐ b. arrested the doctors at the asylum.
   - ____ ☐ c. began spending more money on the mentally ill.

Score 5 points for each correct answer

____ TOTAL SCORE: Recalling Facts

C MAKING INFERENCES

An inference is a judgment that is made or an idea that is arrived at based on facts or on information that is given. You make an inference when you understand something that is *not* stated directly, but that is *implied*, or suggested by the facts that are given.

Below are five statements that are judgments or ideas that have been arrived at from the facts of the story. Write the letter *C* in the box in front of each statement that is a correct inference. Write the letter *F* in front of each faulty inference.

C—Correct Inference   F—Faulty Inference

- ____ ☐ 1. The doctors who declared Nellie insane did not know much about mental illness.

- ____ ☐ 2. If Joseph Pulitzer's lawyer hadn't made arrangements to have Nellie released, she might never have gotten off Blackwells Island.

- ____ ☐ 3. The doctors and nurses at the insane asylum didn't have any respect for people who were mentally ill.

- ____ ☐ 4. Only a very good actress could have fooled the doctors into thinking she was crazy.

- ____ ☐ 5. Nellie Bly was the first person seriously interested in finding out what conditions were like on Blackwells Island.

Score 5 points for each correct answer

____ TOTAL SCORE: Making Inferences

D USING WORDS PRECISELY

Each of the numbered sentences below contains an underlined word or phrase from the story you have just read. Under the sentence are three definitions. One has the *same* meaning as the underlined word or phrase, one has *almost the same* meaning, and one has the *opposite* meaning. Match the definitions with the three answer choices by writing the letter that stands for each answer in the box in front of the definition it goes with.

S—Same   A—Almost the Same   O—Opposite

1. She had expected medical care at the hospital to be <u>minimal</u>, but she was not prepared for the kind of heartless treatment that she saw all around her.

____ ☐ a. the smallest possible amount

____ ☐ b. less than necessary

____ ☐ c. of the highest quality

2. Nellie was equally stunned by the filthy living conditions that <u>prevailed</u> throughout the hospital.

____ ☐ a. were common

____ ☐ b. were rare

____ ☐ c. existed

3. After a couple of days in that <u>inhumane</u> environment, Nellie was ready to get out.

____ ☐ a. unkind

____ ☐ b. caring

____ ☐ c. cruel

4. The story instantly created a <u>scandal</u>, stirring the public's concern for the mentally ill.

____ ☐ a. public disgrace

____ ☐ b. occasion for praise

____ ☐ c. unpleasant situation

5. Nellie went on to write other <u>compelling</u> newspaper reports.

____ ☐ a. interesting

____ ☐ b. dull

____ ☐ c. forceful

____ Score 3 points for each correct *S* answer
____ Score 1 point for each correct *A* or *O* answer

____ TOTAL SCORE: Using Words Precisely

● *Enter the four total scores in the spaces below, and add them together to find your Critical Reading Score. Then record your Critical Reading Score on the graph on page 157.*

```
_____  Finding the Main Idea
_____  Recalling Facts
_____  Making Inferences
_____  Using Words Precisely
_____  CRITICAL READING SCORE: Unit 17
```

It wasn't an easy decision for the Canadian diplomats at the embassy in Iran. Should they take the risk of protecting the six frightened American diplomats from the radical Iranians who hated the United States? They would be putting themselves in great danger. But the Americans had come to them because they had nowhere else to turn. In a courageous gesture of friendship for their neighbors, the Canadians helped the Americans escape from Iran.

The Canadian Embassy: A Risk for Friendship

It began when a woman in one of the front offices screamed, "They're coming over the wall!" It was late in the morning on November 4, 1979. Looking out the window, the Americans in the United States Embassy in Teheran, Iran, saw Iranians swarming into the courtyard. The Iranians ran toward the embassy building, brandishing guns and yelling, "Death to America!"

At first none of the embassy workers could believe what was happening. It was true that a fanatic leader called the Ayatollah Khomeini had recently taken control of Iran, and everyone knew he hated the United States. Still, no one could believe he would allow his people to attack the embassy. International law required governments to protect all embassies on their soil.

By the time the Americans accepted the fact that they really were in danger, it was too late. The radical Iranians broke into the building and took fifty-two Americans hostage. For the next 444 days, the embassy workers were held prisoner inside the embassy. Six other diplomats, however, managed to sneak out a back door and run into the street.

Once out of the building, they did not know what to do. They were not safe anywhere in Iran. If they were spotted, they would be captured or killed. But they had no way of leaving the country. All the airports and train stations were controlled by Iranians who were hostile to Americans.

Desperate, the six diplomats turned to the Canadian Embassy. Would the Canadians help them? It was not a decision that could be made lightly. If the Canadians helped the six Americans, the Iranian radicals would be furious. Iranians might attack the Canadian Embassy and take more hostages. They might even try to kill those who had aided the Americans. On the other hand, could Canada simply stand by and do nothing when its neighbors were in trouble?

Ken Taylor was the Canadian ambassador in Teheran. Quickly he gathered his staff members together and explained the situation. He told them how dangerous it would be to help the fugitives. He emphasized that it would mean putting their lives on the line. Despite the gravity of the situation, the staff workers did not take long to make up their minds. They were unanimous in wanting to do whatever they could to help the Americans.

That was all Ken Taylor needed to know. He devised a plan to hide the six Americans until they could be smuggled out of the country. They would stay in the homes of Canadian diplomats. Taylor himself housed a couple of them. The Canadians could tell no one what they were doing. If word leaked out, the Iranians would try to hunt down the six fugitives and their accomplices.

For more than two months, Taylor and his coworkers harbored the Americans. During that time, Taylor searched for a way to get them safely out of Iran. He found out what documents an international traveler needed. He watched customs officials snoop through the luggage of people crossing the border. He even sent some of his own staff members on unnecessary flights to other nations so they could find out how difficult it was for foreigners to get out of Iran. Those trips also got the Iranians accustomed to seeing Canadians traveling into and out of the country.

Taylor's next move was to ask the Canadian government to issue fake Canadian passports to the six Americans. On January 4, 1980, that bold request was approved. Government officials gave the Americans new identities as Canadian business people who might logically be in Iran on business. Taylor planned to have the Americans use the passports to get out of the country. But he didn't want to rush the plan. He wanted to wait until

Canadian travel patterns out of Iran were more firmly established.

As it turned out, however, Taylor was not able to wait. On January 19, his wife, Patricia, received a phone call.

"May I speak to Mr. or Mrs. Stafford?" the caller asked.

The question terrified Patricia. Joseph and Kathy Stafford were two of the Americans hiding in her house.

"I'm sorry," she said, trying to sound calm. "There is no one by that name living here."

But the caller repeated his request. He said he knew that the Staffords were there.

When Patricia told her husband about the phone call, he decided they would have to hurry. Somebody had discovered that the Canadian diplomats were helping the Americans. Both the Americans and the Canadians were in great danger. They would all have to get out of Iran, and they would have to move fast.

During the next week, Taylor sent many of his coworkers and their families on trips that took them out of Iran. They pretended the trips were for routine embassy business. When the size of the staff was reduced from twenty to four, Taylor was ready to make his move. On Monday, January 28, he sent the six Americans to the Teheran Airport. Pretending to be Canadians traveling on business, they handed their fake passports to the airport officials. They waited anxiously while the Iranians examined the documents. When at last the passports were approved, the Americans boarded a plane to Frankfurt, Germany. On that same day, Taylor and the three other remaining Canadians quietly boarded a plane and flew to Europe.

Within a few days, the Americans rejoined their families in the United States, and the Canadian diplomats made it safely back to Canada. As Taylor had predicted, the government of Iran was enraged when it heard what the Canadian Embassy had done. Iranian officials labeled the Canadians outlaws who had broken the laws of Iran. They even issued threats against Canada. A spokesman for Iran declared, "Sooner or later, somewhere in the world, Canada will pay for this crime."

To Iran, the members of the Canadian Embassy were criminals, but to the rest of the world they were heroes. They had risked their lives to help six frightened Americans escape from the madness in Iran. Americans flooded the Canadian government with thank-you cards. They flew Canadian flags alongside American ones. And billboard owners all across the United States put up giant signs reading, "Thank You, Canada." ■

If you have been timed while reading this selection, enter your reading time below. Then turn to the Words per Minute table on page 155 and look up your reading speed (words per minute). Enter your reading speed on the graph on page 156.

READING TIME: Unit 18

_____ : _____
Minutes   *Seconds*

How well did you read?

- *Answer the four types of questions that follow. The directions for each type of question tell you how to mark your answers.*

- *When you have finished all four exercises, check your work by using the answer key on page 152. For each right answer, put a check mark (✔) on the line beside the box. For each wrong answer, write the correct answer on the line.*

- *For scoring each exercise, follow the directions below the questions.*

A FINDING THE MAIN IDEA

Look at the three statements below. One expresses the main idea of the story you just read. A good main idea statement answers two questions: it tells *who* or *what* is the subject of the story, and it answers the understood question *does what?* or *is what?* Another statement is *too broad*, it is vague and doesn't tell much about the topic of the story. The third statement is *too narrow*, it tells about only one part of the story.

Match the statements with the three answer choices below by writing the letter of each answer in the box in front of the statement it goes with.

M—Main Idea   B—Too Broad   N—Too Narrow

____ ☐ 1. The Canadian Embassy in Iran went out of its way to help endangered members of the United States Embassy.

____ ☐ 2. At great risk, the staff of the Canadian Embassy helped six endangered Americans escape from Iran.

____ ☐ 3. Six Americans were able to escape Iran while fifty-two were held hostage in the United States Embassy.

____ Score 15 points for a correct *M* answer

____ Score 5 points for each correct *B* or *N* answer

____ TOTAL SCORE: Finding the Main Idea

B RECALLING FACTS

How well do you remember the facts in the story you just read? Put an *x* in the box in front of the correct answer to each of the multiple-choice questions below.

1. The fanatic leader of Iran was called
   - ☐ a. Ken Taylor.
   - ☐ b. the Ayatollah Khomeini.
   - ☐ c. Teheran.

2. The Iranians took as hostages
   - ☐ a. 52 Americans.
   - ☐ b. 444 Americans.
   - ☐ c. 6 Americans.

3. The Canadian Embassy hid the Americans for more than
   - ☐ a. two months.
   - ☐ b. four months.
   - ☐ c. five months.

4. The fake passports used by the Americans were issued by
   - ☐ a. the Canadian Embassy.
   - ☐ b. the United States government.
   - ☐ c. the Canadian government.

5. The American diplomats escaped from Iran disguised as Canadian
   - ☐ a. business people.
   - ☐ b. diplomats.
   - ☐ c. tourists.

Score 5 points for each correct answer

_____ TOTAL SCORE: Recalling Facts

C MAKING INFERENCES

An inference is a judgment that is made or an idea that is arrived at based on facts or on information that is given. You make an inference when you understand something that is *not* stated directly, but that is *implied*, or suggested by the facts that are given.

Below are five statements that are judgments or ideas that have been arrived at from the facts of the story. Write the letter *C* in the box in front of each statement that is a correct inference. Write the letter *F* in front of each faulty inference.

C—Correct Inference   F—Faulty Inference

1. Very few governments ever allow their people to attack the embassy of another country.

2. The Ayatollah Khomeini did not feel bound to conduct matters in Iran according to international laws.

3. Any other embassy in Teheran would have done what the Canadians did to help the six Americans.

4. If Patricia Taylor had not received the phone call, her husband would have waited longer before taking the Americans to the airport.

5. Those Americans who were being held hostage were punished for the escape of the six Americans.

Score 5 points for each correct answer

_____ TOTAL SCORE: Making Inferences

D USING WORDS PRECISELY

Each of the numbered sentences below contains an underlined word or phrase from the story you have just read. Under the sentence are three definitions. One has the *same* meaning as the underlined word or phrase, one has *almost the same* meaning, and one has the *opposite* meaning. Match the definitions with the three answer choices by writing the letter that stands for each answer in the box in front of the definition it goes with.

S—Same   A—Almost the Same   O—Opposite

1. All the airports and train stations were controlled by Iranians who were <u>hostile</u> to Americans.

____ ☐ a. sympathetic to

____ ☐ b. unfriendly

____ ☐ c. strongly against

2. Despite the <u>gravity</u> of the situation, the staff workers did not take long to make up their minds.

____ ☐ a. seriousness

____ ☐ b. significance

____ ☐ c. lightness

3. They were <u>unanimous</u> in wanting to do whatever they could to help the Americans.

____ ☐ a. all against

____ ☐ b. all in agreement

____ ☐ c. strongly in favor

4. If word leaked out, the Iranians would try to hunt down the six fugitives and their <u>accomplices</u>.

____ ☐ a. assistants

____ ☐ b. partners in crime

____ ☐ c. enemies

5. For more than two months, Taylor and his coworkers <u>harbored</u> the Americans.

____ ☐ a. sheltered

____ ☐ b. exposed

____ ☐ c. helped

____ Score 3 points for each correct *S* answer

____ Score 1 point for each correct *A* or *O* answer

____ TOTAL SCORE: Using Words Precisely

● *Enter the four total scores in the spaces below, and add them together to find your Critical Reading Score. Then record your Critical Reading Score on the graph on page 157.*

_____	Finding the Main Idea
_____	Recalling Facts
_____	Making Inferences
_____	Using Words Precisely
_____	CRITICAL READING SCORE: Unit 18

Her story has been told many times, but often with more of a romantic gloss than her life and work really held. It is true that Florence Nightingale had great compassion for the sick whom she cared for, but it was her great intelligence and organizational ability, her strength and her hard work that allowed her to raise nursing from a lowly job into an indispensable respectable profession. Through the reforms she instituted, she saved many lives.

Florence Nightingale: A Mission for Life

The screams of wounded soldiers echoed through the corridors. Clogged sewer pipes filled the air with a foul stench. And in every room rats could be seen scurrying from corner to corner, rummaging among the dead bodies that lay scattered on the floor. That was the scene that greeted Florence Nightingale when she arrived at the English army hospital in Scutari, Turkey, on November 9, 1854.

She had gone to take charge of the nursing of soldiers injured in the Crimean War. As England, France and Turkey fought Russia for control of the Black Sea, wounded British soldiers were being sent to Scutari for treatment. But the Scutari Hospital was nothing but a huge old Turkish military barracks that was filthy and underfurnished. Supplies were inadequate, and conditions overall were deplorable. Before Florence arrived, there was no hot water, no soap and no kitchen. There were no clean bandages, no candles or lamps and, worst of all, no nurses.

None of that surprised Florence. She had been warned that the hospital was a shambles. But she had gone to help anyway. She planned to fix up the place and improve care for the wounded. It was a task no one else wanted. In 1854, most people considered nursing to be a dirty business. Only poor, uneducated women became nurses. Most were criminals or alcoholics who agreed to work in a hospital to avoid going to jail. They were totally unfit to care for the sick.

Florence, on the other hand, came from a wealthy London family. She was educated mainly by her father who taught her Greek, Latin, French, German, Italian, history, philosophy and mathematics. As a young girl she spent much time attending parties, concerts and society balls. At the age of seventeen, though, she grew tired of her carefree lifestyle. She longed to devote her energies to something more important. Since she had always been interested in medicine and felt a special sympathy for sick people, she announced her intention to become a nurse.

That announcement shocked Florence's mother. Knowing the awful reputation of nurses, Mrs. Nightingale forbade her daughter to set foot in a hospital. For the next sixteen years, Florence honored her mother's wishes, but she did not put aside her interest in the care of the sick. She educated herself by reading books and reports on medicine and public health. Then in 1850 she took a full nurses' training course at a school in Germany. By 1853 she knew more about caring for the sick than any nurse in the country.

Although her mother still objected, Florence decided that the time had come to put her knowledge to use. In August she became head of a women's hospital in London. There she surprised the doctors by listening to the complaints and criticisms of the patients. She instituted reforms throughout the hospital and tried to provide the nurses with some basic training.

Florence was working there when the Crimean War broke out. When Sidney Herbert, the British Secretary of War, heard of the appalling conditions at Scutari Hospital, he knew something had to be done. Someone had to clean up the facilities there and organize proper care for the wounded. Herbert could think of only one person for the job: Florence Nightingale.

Herbert wrote to Florence, urging her to go to Scutari. Although her friends tried to discourage her, Florence readily agreed to go. She could not ignore the needs of the brave men who were fighting for their country. Rounding up thirty-eight trained nurses to accompany her, she set off for Turkey.

When she arrived at the hospital, Florence expected a warm welcome from the doctors. Instead they were cool—even hostile. They were angry that the Secretary of War had sent a woman to interfere with their routine. They thought that Florence was nothing more than some fragile, high-bred woman who would be of no help to them at all.

It didn't take Florence long to prove the doctors wrong. On the day she arrived, five hundred wounded cavalry soldiers were brought in from a battle that had just been fought. The doctors worked frantically to treat the most severely wounded. Many men had been shot in the arm or the leg and needed to have the injured limb amputated before infection set in. Having no way to dispose of the severed limbs, the doctors simply threw them out the window. As the rotting arms and legs piled up in the hospital courtyard, the other nurses just stared in horror. But Florence quickly went to work. She found a hospital attendant with an old army cart and arranged to have the pile hauled away and buried.

Over the next few days Florence set up three kitchens and a laundry. She also organized a cleaning crew to scrub the entire building. Using her own money, she bought bandages, sheets, operating tables, pots and pans, lamps, towels and silver-ware. This was the first time in history that wounded soldiers received good hospital care.

Florence herself assisted doctors even during the bloodiest operations. And she never avoided patients with contagious diseases. She knew she was risking her own health by having contact with those soldiers. Still, she spent hours by their bedsides, nursing them back to health. "She was so brave herself," one soldier said, "she gave us all courage."

Before long Florence had won the admiration of every patient in the hospital. Despite her hectic schedule, she always found time to visit the wards where the soldiers slept. Usually she went at night when she had finished the rest of her work. To light her way along the four miles of corridors, she carried a small lamp. The soldiers loved to see her coming. Many were young boys, only fifteen or sixteen years old, and often they were in too much pain to sleep. As they lay in the dark and lonely ward, they watched for the woman they called "The Lady with the Lamp." "What comfort we felt to see her," one soldier said. "We kissed her shadow as she passed."

Florence was so successful in organizing the Scutari Hospital that she was put in charge of all the British army hospitals in the Crimea. When the Crimean War ended in 1856, Florence returned to England a national hero. But she did not want public acclaim. She established a quiet, private life devoted to further work in the field of health care.

But her years in Turkey had taken their toll. The hard work and constant exposure to disease had permanently weakened her health. Within a few years of her return to England, she was an invalid. But that did not stop her from working. She wrote several books and founded a school for nurses. She took care of her correspondence, research and writing from a couch in her London home. She also received many visitors. She was considered an authority on the care of the sick, and her advice was sought by important people the world over. The United States even asked her advice for setting up field hospitals during the Civil War.

Florence Nightingale accomplished a great deal in her life. She single-handedly transformed nursing from a lowly, unskilled job into a respectable, even noble, profession. She established an efficient and compassionate system for caring for the sick. And she won the undying gratitude of hundreds of thousands of young English soldiers. In 1907, Florence Nightingale was awarded the British Order of Merit. She was the first woman ever to receive that honor. ■

If you have been timed while reading this selection, enter your reading time below. Then turn to the Words per Minute table on page 155 and look up your reading speed (words per minute). Enter your reading speed on the graph on page 156.

How well did you read?

- *Answer the four types of questions that follow. The directions for each type of question tell you how to mark your answers.*

- *When you have finished all four exercises, check your work by using the answer key on page 152. For each right answer, put a check mark (✔) on the line beside the box. For each wrong answer, write the correct answer on the line.*

- *For scoring each exercise, follow the directions below the questions.*

A FINDING THE MAIN IDEA

Look at the three statements below. One expresses the main idea of the story you just read. A good main idea statement answers two questions: it tells *who* or *what* is the subject of the story, and it answers the understood question *does what?* or *is what?* Another statement is *too broad*, it is vague and doesn't tell much about the topic of the story. The third statement is *too narrow*, it tells about only one part of the story.

Match the statements with the three answer choices below by writing the letter of each answer in the box in front of the statement it goes with.

M—Main Idea   **B—Too Broad**   **N—Too Narrow**

_____ ☐ 1. Against the wishes of her upper-class family, Florence Nightingale studied health care and turned nursing into a scientific profession.

_____ ☐ 2. Florence Nightingale worked in a hospital for British soldiers in Turkey during the Crimean War and forever changed the way people looked at nurses.

_____ ☐ 3. Florence Nightingale's courage, organizational ability and hard work greatly improved the way wounded soldiers were cared for and made nursing an honorable profession.

_____ Score 15 points for a correct *M* answer

_____ Score 5 points for each correct *B* or *N* answer

_____ TOTAL SCORE: Finding the Main Idea

B RECALLING FACTS

How well do you remember the facts in the story you just read? Put an *x* in the box in front of the correct answer to each of the multiple-choice questions below.

1. In the early 1800s, most English nurses were
   - ____ ☐ a. well trained.
   - ____ ☐ b. criminals or alcoholics.
   - ____ ☐ c. in Turkey caring for soldiers wounded in the Crimean War.

2. When Florence first announced her intention to become a nurse, her mother
   - ____ ☐ a. enrolled her in a school for nurses.
   - ____ ☐ b. sent her to Scutari to study medicine.
   - ____ ☐ c. forbade her to set foot in a hospital.

3. Before going to Turkey, Florence
   - ____ ☐ a. spent time in a London hospital.
   - ____ ☐ b. knew nothing about medicine or public health.
   - ____ ☐ c. was head of a women's hospital.

4. When Florence arrived at Scutari Hospital, the doctors
   - ____ ☐ a. were unfriendly.
   - ____ ☐ b. gave her a warm welcome.
   - ____ ☐ c. were not doing anything for the wounded.

5. The Scutari Hospital was
   - ____ ☐ a. a training place for nurses.
   - ____ ☐ b. a Turkish barracks.
   - ____ ☐ c. an old factory.

Score 5 points for each correct answer

____ TOTAL SCORE: Recalling Facts

C MAKING INFERENCES

An inference is a judgment that is made or an idea that is arrived at based on facts or on information that is given. You make an inference when you understand something that is *not* stated directly, but that is *implied* or suggested by the facts that are given.

Below are five statements that are judgments or ideas that have been arrived at from the facts of the story. Write the letter C in the box in front of each statement that is a correct inference. Write the letter F in front of each faulty inference.

C—Correct Inference   F—Faulty Inference

- ____ ☐ 1. Florence Nightingale was an extremely good manager.

- ____ ☐ 2. Before Florence Nightingale began changing the way nurses were trained, nursing was not considered an important function.

- ____ ☐ 3. The doctors at Scutari Hospital did not care whether the soldiers in their care lived or died.

- ____ ☐ 4. Because of her decision to go into nursing, Florence Nightingale was rejected by upper-class British society.

- ____ ☐ 5. If it hadn't been for the Crimean War, Florence would not have become concerned about the health care of soldiers.

Score 5 points for each correct answer

____ TOTAL SCORE: Making Inferences

D USING WORDS PRECISELY

Each of the numbered sentences below contains an underlined word or phrase from the story you have just read. Under the sentence are three definitions. One has the *same* meaning as the underlined word or phrase, one has *almost the same* meaning, and one has the *opposite* meaning. Match the definitions with the three answer choices by writing the letter that stands for each answer in the box in front of the definition it goes with.

S—Same   A—Almost the Same   O—Opposite

1. For the next sixteen years, Florence <u>honored</u> her mother's wishes, but she did not put aside her interest in the care of the sick.

____ ☐ a. fulfilled

____ ☐ b. abided by

____ ☐ c. went against

2. She <u>instituted</u> reforms throughout the hospital and tried to provide the nurses with some basic training.

____ ☐ a. invented

____ ☐ b. did away with

____ ☐ c. established

3. Having no way to dispose of the <u>severed</u> limbs, the doctors simply threw them out the window.

____ ☐ a. mended

____ ☐ b. broken

____ ☐ c. cut off

4. When Sidney Herbert, the British Secretary of War, heard of the <u>appalling</u> conditions at Scutari Hospital, he knew something had to be done.

____ ☐ a. dreadful

____ ☐ b. offensive

____ ☐ c. appealing

5. Florence returned to England a national hero. But she did not want public <u>acclaim</u>.

____ ☐ a. praise

____ ☐ b. congratulations

____ ☐ c. disgrace

____ Score 3 points for each correct *S* answer

____ Score 1 point for each correct *A* or *O* answer

____ TOTAL SCORE: Using Words Precisely

● *Enter the four total scores in the spaces below, and add them together to find your Critical Reading Score. Then record your Critical Reading Score on the graph on page 157.*

_____ Finding the Main Idea
_____ Recalling Facts
_____ Making Inferences
_____ Using Words Precisely
_____ CRITICAL READING SCORE: Unit 19

Held as a prisoner of war by the North Vietnamese for almost seven and a half years, James Bond Stockdale never gave up hope. In fact, he inspired it in his fellow prisoners. Through the pain of torture and the desolation of solitary confinement, he never relinquished his faith in life and his fellow man.

James Bond Stockdale: Prisoner of War

On the morning of September 9, 1965, Commander James Bond Stockdale climbed into his A-4 Navy jet. He had orders to carry out another bombing mission. He was supposed to fly his jet from an aircraft carrier in the South China Sea to a target in North Vietnam. It was a dangerous mission because the target was deep in enemy territory. At age forty-one, he had already flown more than two hundred combat missions into North Vietnam. He was committed to helping the United States and South Vietnam crush the communists of North Vietnam. This flight, however, would be his last mission as a combat pilot.

Stockdale flew to his target and dropped his bombs. Then he heard gunfire; his plane had been hit. Red lights on the control panel began flashing wildly. The jet was going down. Stockdale's only hope was to eject and parachute into enemy territory. He quickly bailed out. The North Vietnamese soldiers saw his parachute open and rushed to capture him. James Bond Stockdale now faced the greatest challenge of his life.

For the next 2,714 days, nearly seven and a half years, Stockdale was a prisoner of the North Vietnamese. He was held in the Hoa Lo (Fiery Furnace) prison, nicknamed the "Hanoi Hilton" by the prisoners of war (POWs).

What Stockdale and the other POWs had to endure is hard for most people to imagine. They were frequently tortured by their North Vietnamese captors. They were put in leg irons, beaten, and denied food. They were locked in separate cells so they could not talk to one another. Sometimes they were forced to go without sleep for long periods of time. Through such inhumane tactics, the North Vietnamese hoped to break the spirits of the POWs so that they would give away military secrets. The North Vietnamese also encouraged POWs to spy on one another and to confess to crimes they hadn't committed. Such confessions would make great propaganda.

Stockdale's captors were especially rough with him because he was the top-ranking officer among the prisoners. They were sure that if they could get him to cooperate the other prisoners would follow suit. So they developed a special "persuasion" program for him. They questioned him daily. When he refused to talk, they punched, whipped and kicked him. They tied ropes around his arms and pulled them tighter and tighter until no blood could flow to his hands. They tried

to force him to sign false confessions. They wanted him to say that the United States was bombing innocent North Vietnamese people in churches and schools. They wanted him to beg for their forgiveness.

But Stockdale held out. Even when the torture became agonizing, he refused to submit to the demands of his captors. His was an incredible display of willpower. The North Vietnamese were not accustomed to such bravery. They grew more and more frustrated. During one session they beat him so brutally that his leg was broken. Still he would not give in.

At one point during his captivity, Stockdale felt that his resolve was beginning to crack. As the torture and the questioning continued, he feared that he was on the verge of giving up secrets. To prevent that from happening, he jumped up and ran to the small window in the cell. While his startled captors watched, he grabbed a stool and hurled it through the window. He then began stabbing his wrists with a piece of broken glass. The floor was soon covered with blood. The horrified guards finally stopped their questioning.

Stockdale was later asked why he had done such a thing to himself. He said, "I felt the only way I could really deter and stop this flow of questions was to show a commitment to death. I don't think that I intended to die, but I intended to make them think that I was ready to die." For his action, Stockdale was later awarded the Medal of Honor.

On another occasion, in 1969, the North Vietnamese wanted to use Stockdale in a propaganda film. They wanted the film to show the world that the POWs were being treated well. Again Stockdale refused to cooperate. He would not allow himself to be a party to such an obvious lie. So he took a wooden stool and smashed his face with it several times. When he stopped, his face was covered with puffy bruises. Next he found a razor blade and chopped away at his hair, leaving bloody scars on his scalp. His plan worked. The North Vietnamese could not use a battered prisoner in their propaganda film.

After a while, the North Vietnamese tried a softer approach. They asked Stockdale to be reasonable. They promised him that he would get better treatment. But being "reasonable" meant betraying his fellow prisoners. It meant reporting other POWs to the guards if they broke any rules. It meant sending those prisoners off to be tortured. And it meant setting an example that would weaken the will-power of other prisoners. Stockdale refused to be reasonable. "The object of our highest moral value was the well-being of our fellow prisoners," he later said. "You are your brother's keeper."

To help unify the prisoners in the camp, Stockdale organized a resistance movement. He set up a communications network. He devised a code so the men could tap messages to each other on the walls between their cells. If a prisoner was caught tapping on the wall, it meant certain torture. But the contact was worth the risk to the lonely men. They had to communicate. They had to comfort each other and keep each other from despair.

Under such terrible conditions, the bond between prisoners can become powerful. According to Stockdale, "Your fellow prisoners are the most precious thing on earth and deserve your care no matter what the risk. You become unashamed to say what you mean when your pal is being taken out for torture for being caught trying to get a message to you. You tap, 'God bless you, Jerry' or perhaps, 'I love you, Jerry.'" When asked what kept him going during those seven and a half years of imprisonment, Stockdale said simply, "The men next door."

It is amazing that Stockdale survived in the "Hanoi Hilton" for such a long time. His heroism lies in the fact that he did more than survive. He won. He beat his enemies by always refusing to give in to them. And he paid a terrible price. His left leg was permanently damaged. His weight dropped to barely a hundred pounds. For three years he was kept in solitary confinement, which meant that he could not see any of his fellow prisoners. And during the entire seven and a half years,

he had no communication with his family. Had his wife and sons given up hope?

Finally, in February 1973, the United States made a deal with North Vietnam. On February 12, Stockdale and 115 other Americans were released from the prison. They were the first Americans to walk out of the Hanoi prison. When Stockdale reached home, he found that his family had not given up hope. But the seven and a half years had not been easy for them either. Stockdale's wife, for example, had suffered two nervous breakdowns. But at last the nightmare was over.

Today Stockdale is once again healthy and vigorous. His stiff left leg is the only visible reminder of his long ordeal. He now teaches history and philosophy at Stanford University in California. He also teaches his students how to hold on to their beliefs and principles, even under pressure. It is a subject in which he is a true expert. ■

If you have been timed while reading this selection, enter your reading time below. Then turn to the Words per Minute table on page 155 and look up your reading speed (words per minute). Enter your reading speed on the graph on page 156.

READING TIME: Unit 20

_____ : _____
Minutes   *Seconds*

How well did you read?

- *Answer the four types of questions that follow. The directions for each type of question tell you how to mark your answers.*

- *When you have finished all four exercises, check your work by using the answer key on page 152. For each right answer, put a check mark (✓) on the line beside the box. For each wrong answer, write the correct answer on the line.*

- *For scoring each exercise, follow the directions below the questions.*

A FINDING THE MAIN IDEA

Look at the three statements below. One expresses the main idea of the story you just read. A good main idea statement answers two questions: it tells *who* or *what* is the subject of the story, and it answers the understood question *does what?* or *is what?* Another statement is *too broad*, it is vague and doesn't tell much about the topic of the story. The third statement is *too narrow*, it tells about only one part of the story.

Match the statements with the three answer choices below by writing the letter of each answer in the box in front of the statement it goes with.

M—Main Idea   **B—Too Broad**   **N—Too Narrow**

_____ ☐ 1. Commander James Bond Stockdale was a United States navy pilot who showed extreme courage and strength in Vietnam during the Vietnam War.

_____ ☐ 2. James Bond Stockdale showed that he had the courage and the willingness to take his own life rather than reveal secrets to the enemy.

_____ ☐ 3. James Bond Stockdale remained strong through seven and a half years as a prisoner of the North Vietnamese, and helped his fellow prisoners stay strong too.

_____ Score 15 points for a correct *M* answer
_____ Score 5 points for each correct *B* or *N* answer

_____ TOTAL SCORE: Finding the Main Idea

B RECALLING FACTS

How well do you remember the facts in the story you just read?
Put an x in the box in front of the correct answer to each of the
multiple-choice questions below.

1. Stockdale's A-4 jet was shot down
   - ____ ☐ a. as he entered enemy territory.
   - ____ ☐ b. just before he dropped his bombs.
   - ____ ☐ c. just after he dropped his bombs.

2. The North Vietnamese wanted to break down
   Stockdale's resistance because he
   - ____ ☐ a. was very stubborn.
   - ____ ☐ b. believed in the Vietnam War.
   - ____ ☐ c. was a top-ranking officer among the POWs.

3. The North Vietnamese decided not to use Stockdale
   in a propaganda film because
   - ____ ☐ a. he did not speak Vietnamese.
   - ____ ☐ b. he looked beaten and mistreated.
   - ____ ☐ c. he was about to be released.

4. Prisoners at the "Hanoi Hilton" tapped on the walls
   of their cells to
   - ____ ☐ a. call the guards.
   - ____ ☐ b. send messages to fellow prisoners.
   - ____ ☐ c. annoy the North Vietnamese.

5. During his imprisonment, the most important thing
   to Stockdale was
   - ____ ☐ a. having a chance to sleep.
   - ____ ☐ b. regular meals.
   - ____ ☐ c. his fellow prisoners.

Score 5 points for each correct answer

____ TOTAL SCORE: Recalling Facts

C MAKING INFERENCES

An inference is a judgment that is made or an idea that is
arrived at based on facts or on information that is given. You
make an inference when you understand something that is *not*
stated directly, but that is *implied*, or suggested by the facts that
are given.

Below are five statements that are judgments or ideas that
have been arrived at from the facts of the story. Write the letter
C in the box in front of each statement that is a correct inference. Write the letter F in front of each faulty inference.

C—Correct Inference   F—Faulty Inference

- ____ ☐ 1. The North Vietnamese thought it was important
   to get the POWs to confess to crimes.

- ____ ☐ 2. Being "reasonable" meant the same thing to
   Stockdale that it did to the North Vietnamese.

- ____ ☐ 3. The seven and a half years that Stockdale spent
   as a POW made it impossible for him to adjust
   to normal life after his release.

- ____ ☐ 4. During his captivity James Stockdale did not care
   about his own life.

- ____ ☐ 5. Lack of communication weakened the will and
   the strength of the men.

Score 5 points for each correct answer

____ TOTAL SCORE: Making Inferences

D USING WORDS PRECISELY

Each of the numbered sentences below contains an underlined word or phrase from the story you have just read. Under the sentence are three definitions. One has the *same* meaning as the underlined word or phrase, one has *almost the same* meaning, and one has the *opposite* meaning. Match the definitions with the three answer choices by writing the letter that stands for each answer in the box in front of the definition it goes with.

S—Same   A—Almost the Same   O—Opposite

1. They were put in leg irons, beaten, and <u>denied</u> food.

____ ☐ a. given very little

____ ☐ b. deprived of

____ ☐ c. given

2. They were sure that if they could get him to cooperate the other prisoners would <u>follow suit</u>.

____ ☐ a. do the same thing

____ ☐ b. think of repeating his actions

____ ☐ c. do what they pleased

3. He would not allow himself to be <u>a party to</u> such an obvious lie.

____ ☐ a. a participant in an action

____ ☐ b. a person who refuses to take part

____ ☐ c. a person who believes in something

4. At one point during his captivity, Stockdale felt that his <u>resolve</u> was beginning to crack.

____ ☐ a. strength

____ ☐ b. lack of purpose

____ ☐ c. determination

5. Under such terrible conditions, the <u>bond</u> between prisoners can become powerful.

____ ☐ a. tie

____ ☐ b. sympathy

____ ☐ c. separateness

____ Score 3 points for each correct *S* answer
____ Score 1 point for each correct *A* or *O* answer

____ TOTAL SCORE: Using Words Precisely

● *Enter the four total scores in the spaces below, and add them together to find your Critical Reading Score. Then record your Critical Reading Score on the graph on page 157.*

_____ Finding the Main Idea
_____ Recalling Facts
_____ Making Inferences
_____ Using Words Precisely

_____ CRITICAL READING SCORE: Unit 20

Brother and sister, Hans and Sophie Scholl were united in their determination to do everything in their power to stop Hitler's insanity. Through pamphlets printed and distributed in secret, they spread the word of his crimes against the Jews. They hoped to rouse other people to protest. Such freedom of expression was, of course, not allowed by the Nazis. So when Hans and Sophie were caught, their voices were silenced.

Hans and Sophie Scholl: Resisting Nazi Terror

Hans and Sophie Scholl were ordinary children. They didn't plan on becoming heroes. Hans was born in 1918, and his sister Sophie in 1921. They spent their childhood playing in the fields of a small German town where their father was mayor. They were happy children and looked forward to a bright future. Their dreams were simple: Sophie wanted to be a kindergarten teacher, and Hans hoped to be a doctor. But life did not stay simple for Hans and Sophie. Germany was changing in the 1930s, and the changes were to alter the lives of both Sophie and Hans.

First came the rise of Adolf Hitler and the Nazi Party. Hitler promised to make Germany great. He promised to create new jobs, unite the German people, and restore pride in the fatherland. Those promises sounded so appealing that most people supported Hitler and his Nazi Party. But Hitler had other, less glorious, goals that many people did not know about at first. He believed that the German people were the best and the smartest on earth. And though that might sound like simple pride in his people, it was part of a twisted view of humanity. It was coupled with a belief that everyone else was inferior, and that they should be controlled by the Germans. He also had an irrational hatred for certain people, the Jews in particular. He

began an organized program to wipe all Jews from the face of the earth.

Hitler expected all Germans to agree with him. He wanted everyone to share his warped dream. To teach the German children his ideas, he set up an organization called the Hitler Youth. At first the organization seemed much like America's Boy Scouts and Girl Scouts. Troops of Hitler Youth sang songs, learned crafts and took hikes through the German countryside. Soon, however, the leaders of the group demanded that all members become Nazis. Children in the organization were no longer allowed to sing their own songs or carry their own handmade flags. They could sing only Nazi songs and carry only Hitler's flag.

Like many young Germans, Sophie and Hans Scholl joined the Hitler Youth. But gradually they began to see the evil of the Nazi movement. They began to pull away from the group and to speak out against it. Because of his protests against the group, Hans was sent to prison for a little while in 1938. By that time the dark side of Hitler's plan was clear to both Hans and Sophie.

In 1939, Hans left for the University of Munich to study medicine. Sophie joined him in 1942 as a student of biology and philosophy. In Munich, the Scholls met

others who hated what Hitler was doing. They learned that Hitler had set up concentration camps for Jews. Hitler's soldiers were rounding up all the Jews they could find and shipping them off to the camps, where they were starved, tortured and killed. As Hans and Sophie talked with other students, they arrived at a decision: they had to do something to try to stop Hitler. They believed that any person who did not actively resist the Nazis had to share the guilt for Hitler's deeds. To do nothing was to allow the terror to continue.

And so the White Rose was born. Working with a few close friends, Hans and Sophie created the White Rose, a secret resistance group. Their goal was to spread the word of Hitler's crimes against the Jews and so rouse other students to protest. It was a dangerous undertaking. The Nazis would not tolerate any resistance. They would imprison or kill anyone who disagreed with their policies.

Nevertheless, Hans managed to get his hands on a printing press, and the group began their activities. Working at night in the basement of Hans and Sophie's apartment, they put together a series of four pamphlets called the Leaflets of the White Rose. Each leaflet urged the German people to rise up against Hitler.

It was dangerous enough to write and print the leaflets, but it was even more dangerous to distribute them. Nazi soldiers were positioned throughout the city and were free to stop anyone they chose. Soldiers often demanded to be allowed to search a bag, a suitcase or even a person's body. If anything suspicious was found, the person might be whisked off to a concentration camp for questioning and possible torture.

Despite the great risk involved, it was often Sophie or Hans who volunteered to pack a suitcase with leaflets and carry it out into the city. Sometimes Hans left leaflets in an empty classroom at the university. Sometimes Sophie moved quietly through the streets in the early morning hours, slipping one leaflet into each mailbox she passed. Sometimes Hans and Sophie even took trains to other cities in the hope that the resistance would spread beyond Munich.

The leaflets produced by the White Rose caused a lot of excitement at the university. In fact, throughout the city people began to whisper about the bold pamphlets. So as Sophie and Hans hoped, the resistance did spread to other cities. The leaflets were reprinted by students in Hamburg and eventually made their way to England, where they were copied by the thousands.

Meanwhile, the Nazis were moving in on the Scholls. February 18, 1943 was a beautiful sunny morning. Hans and Sophie left their apartment together and headed for the university. They had with them a suitcase full of the forbidden leaflets. They reached the university and quickly scattered the leaflets around the campus. But this time they were spotted, and within minutes the German police had arrested them both.

Hans and Sophie knew that the Nazis would probably show them no mercy. The White Rose was a symbol of freedom, and that was exactly what Hitler was trying to destroy. Thus Sophie was not surprised when the endless hours of questioning began. For two days and two nights Sophie was grilled by Nazi officials. In a separate room, Hans was suffering the same treatment.

At first Sophie and Hans denied everything. But when it became clear that the Nazis had proof of their illegal actions, Sophie and Hans reversed their story. They took the blame for everything that the White Rose had done. They insisted that they were the only people who knew anything about the leaflets. Sophie and Hans were trying to protect the other members of the resistance group.

Confessing to the crimes was an act of courage. If the Scholls had denied the charges, or if they had given the names of other White Rose members, their lives might have been spared. But now the Nazis would surely put them to death. Still, Sophie and Hans remained calm, brave and unwavering in their contempt for Hitler. The Nazi officials had never seen anything like it. Not once did Sophie or Hans apologize or ask for forgiveness. They believed in their cause. Their spirits could not be broken.

On Sunday afternoon, three days after the arrest, the Nazis stopped questioning the Scholls. The police had made their decision. Hans and Sophie would be executed the very next day. With death only a few hours away, the Scholls still retained their composure. They both slept soundly that night, for their consciences were clear. Sophie and Hans had not stopped Hitler, but their actions had helped awaken the world to his crimes.

When Sophie walked to the executioner's block the next day, she held her head high. She died quietly, with dignity. Her brother Hans showed similar courage. His final words before the ax fell were, "Long live freedom!" ∎

If you have been timed while reading this selection, enter your reading time below. Then turn to the Words per Minute table on page 155 and look up your reading speed (words per minute). Enter your reading speed on the graph on page 156.

READING TIME: Unit 21

_____ : _____
Minutes   Seconds

How well did you read?

- *Answer the four types of questions that follow. The directions for each type of question tell you how to mark your answers.*

- *When you have finished all four exercises, check your work by using the answer key on page 152. For each right answer, put a check mark (✔) on the line beside the box. For each wrong answer, write the correct answer on the line.*

- *For scoring each exercise, follow the directions below the questions.*

A FINDING THE MAIN IDEA

Look at the three statements below. One expresses the main idea of the story you just read. A good main idea statement answers two questions: it tells *who* or *what* is the subject of the story, and it answers the understood question *does what?* or *is what?* Another statement is *too broad*, it is vague and doesn't tell much about the topic of the story. The third statement is *too narrow*, it tells about only one part of the story.

Match the statements with the three answer choices below by writing the letter of each answer in the box in front of the statement it goes with.

M—Main Idea   B—Too Broad   N—Too Narrow

_____ ☐ 1. Sophie and Hans Scholl were German students who distributed many leaflets against the Nazis.

_____ ☐ 2. Sophie and Hans Scholl acted with great courage and conviction in an effort to educate the world about the Nazis.

_____ ☐ 3. Sophie and Hans Scholl were German students who risked their lives and finally died trying to alert the world to the evils of Adolf Hitler.

_____ Score 15 points for a correct *M* answer
_____ Score 5 points for each correct *B* or *N* answer

_____ TOTAL SCORE: Finding the Main Idea

B RECALLING FACTS

How well do you remember the facts in the story you just read? Put an *x* in the box in front of the correct answer to each of the multiple-choice questions below.

1. As children, Hans and Sophie Scholl were
   - ____ ☐ a. members of the Hitler Youth.
   - ____ ☐ b. members of the Boy Scouts and Girl Scouts.
   - ____ ☐ c. unhappy living in Germany.

2. The leaflets of the White Rose were printed in
   - ____ ☐ a. a classroom at the University of Munich.
   - ____ ☐ b. the basement of the Scholls' apartment.
   - ____ ☐ c. Hans and Sophie's hometown.

3. Members of the White Rose sometimes distributed leaflets by
   - ____ ☐ a. mailing them to students in other cities.
   - ____ ☐ b. handing them out to people on street corners.
   - ____ ☐ c. slipping them into mailboxes.

4. When captured, Sophie and Hans took responsibility for printing the leaflets because they
   - ____ ☐ a. wanted to protect the other members of the White Rose.
   - ____ ☐ b. were afraid of being tortured.
   - ____ ☐ c. were hoping the Nazis would be merciful.

5. Four days after Hans and Sophie were arrested,
   - ____ ☐ a. Sophie finally gave police the names of all White Rose members.
   - ____ ☐ b. they apologized for what they had done.
   - ____ ☐ c. they were executed.

Score 5 points for each correct answer

____ TOTAL SCORE: Recalling Facts

C MAKING INFERENCES

An inference is a judgment that is made or an idea that is arrived at based on facts or on information that is given. You make an inference when you understand something that is *not* stated directly, but that is *implied*, or suggested by the facts that are given.

Below are five statements that are judgments or ideas that have been arrived at from the facts of the story. Write the letter *C* in the box in front of each statement that is a correct inference. Write the letter *F* in front of each faulty inference.

C—Correct Inference   F—Faulty Inference

- ____ ☐ 1. The other members of the White Rose were eventually caught and executed too.
- ____ ☐ 2. Sophie and Hans volunteered to distribute the leaflets because they liked taking risks.
- ____ ☐ 3. The execution of Hans and Sophie ended all resistance to Hitler in Germany.
- ____ ☐ 4. Sophie and Hans were more interested in standing up for their ideals than they were in saving their own lives.
- ____ ☐ 5. Nazi officials expected their prisoners to break down and beg for mercy.

Score 5 points for each correct answer

____ TOTAL SCORE: Making Inferences

D USING WORDS PRECISELY

Each of the numbered sentences below contains an underlined word or phrase from the story you have just read. Under the sentence are three definitions. One has the *same* meaning as the underlined word or phrase, one has *almost the same* meaning, and one has the *opposite* meaning. Match the definitions with the three answer choices by writing the letter that stands for each answer in the box in front of the definition it goes with.

S—Same   A—Almost the Same   O—Opposite

1. They believed that any person who did not actively resist the Nazis had to share the guilt for Hitler's deeds.

____ ☐ a. act against

____ ☐ b. express disapproval of

____ ☐ c. support

2. Their goal was to spread the word of Hitler's crimes against the Jews and so rouse other students to protest.

____ ☐ a. stir

____ ☐ b. turn off

____ ☐ c. encourage

3. The Nazis would not tolerate any resistance.

____ ☐ a. forbid

____ ☐ b. allow

____ ☐ c. put up with

4. Still, Sophie and Hans remained calm, brave and unwavering in their contempt for Hitler.

____ ☐ a. persistent

____ ☐ b. uncertain

____ ☐ c. steady

5. With death only a few hours away, the Scholls still retained their composure.

____ ☐ a. self-control

____ ☐ b. nervousness

____ ☐ c. quiet nature

____ Score 3 points for each correct S answer
____ Score 1 point for each correct A or O answer

____ TOTAL SCORE: Using Words Precisely

● *Enter the four total scores in the spaces below, and add them together to find your Critical Reading Score. Then record your Critical Reading Score on the graph on page 157.*

_____ Finding the Main Idea
_____ Recalling Facts
_____ Making Inferences
_____ Using Words Precisely

_____ CRITICAL READING SCORE: Unit 21

ANSWER KEY

1 Wilma Rudolph: Against the Odds

A. Finding the Main Idea
1. **N**   2. **M**   3. **B**

B. Recalling Facts
1. **c**   2. **a**   3. **b**   4. **a**   5. **c**

C. Making Inferences
1. **F**   2. **C**   3. **C**   4. **F**   5. **C**

D. Using Words Precisely
1. a. **A**   b. **S**   c. **O**
2. a. **A**   b. **O**   c. **S**
3. a. **O**   b. **A**   c. **S**
4. a. **S**   b. **O**   c. **A**
5. a. **A**   b. **S**   c. **O**

2 The Four Chaplains

A. Finding the Main Idea
1. **N**   2. **M**   3. **B**

B. Recalling Facts
1. **c**   2. **a**   3. **b**   4. **b**   5. **b**

C. Making Inferences
1. **F**   2. **C**   3. **F**   4. **C**   5. **C**

D. Using Words Precisely
1. a. **S**   b. **O**   c. **A**
2. a. **A**   b. **O**   c. **S**
3. a. **A**   b. **S**   c. **O**
4. a. **O**   b. **A**   c. **S**
5. a. **S**   b. **O**   c. **A**

3 Jackie Robinson: The Loneliest Season

A. Finding the Main Idea
1. **N**   2. **B**   3. **M**

B. Recalling Facts
1. **a**   2. **b**   3. **a**   4. **a**   5. **b**

C. Making Inferences
1. **F**   2. **C**   3. **F**   4. **F**   5. **C**

D. Using Words Precisely
1. a. **S**   b. **O**   c. **A**
2. a. **A**   b. **S**   c. **O**
3. a. **S**   b. **A**   c. **O**
4. a. **S**   b. **O**   c. **A**
5. a. **O**   b. **A**   c. **S**

4 Cesar Chavez: Uniting Farm Workers

A. Finding the Main Idea
1. **M**   2. **B**   3. **N**

B. Recalling Facts
1. **c**   2. **c**   3. **b**   4. **b**   5. **c**

C. Making Inferences
1. **F**   2. **F**   3. **C**   4. **C**   5. **F**

D. Using Words Precisely
1. a. **O**   b. **A**   c. **S**
2. a. **S**   b. **A**   c. **O**
3. a. **O**   b. **A**   c. **S**
4. a. **A**   b. **O**   c. **S**
5. a. **A**   b. **O**   c. **S**

5 Terry Fox and the Marathon of Hope

A. Finding the Main Idea
1. **M**   2. **B**   3. **N**

B. Recalling Facts
1. **a**   2. **c**   3. **c**   4. **b**   5. **c**

C. Making Inferences
1. **C**   2. **F**   3. **C**   4. **F**   5. **C**

D. Using Words Precisely
1. a. **S**   b. **A**   c. **O**
2. a. **O**   b. **S**   c. **A**
3. a. **S**   b. **O**   c. **A**
4. a. **O**   b. **S**   c. **A**
5. a. **O**   b. **A**   c. **S**

6 Mahatma Gandhi: The Peaceful Way

A. Finding the Main Idea
1. **B**   2. **M**   3. **N**

B. Recalling Facts
1. **a**   2. **c**   3. **c**   4. **a**   5. **b**

C. Making Inferences
1. **C**   2. **F**   3. **C**   4. **C**   5. **C**

D. Using Words Precisely
1. a. **O**   b. **S**   c. **A**
2. a. **S**   b. **O**   c. **A**
3. a. **A**   b. **O**   c. **S**
4. a. **S**   b. **O**   c. **A**
5. a. **O**   b. **A**   c. **S**

7 Gladys Aylward: Journey to Safety

A. Finding the Main Idea
1. **M**   2. **B**   3. **N**

B. Recalling Facts
1. **b**   2. **b**   3. **a**   4. **c**   5. **c**

C. Making Inferences
1. **C**   2. **C**   3. **F**   4. **F**   5. **F**

D. Using Words Precisely
1. a. **S**   b. **O**   c. **A**
2. a. **A**   b. **S**   c. **O**
3. a. **S**   b. **A**   c. **O**
4. a. **A**   b. **O**   c. **S**
5. a. **O**   b. **A**   c. **S**

8 Matthew Henson:
To the Top of the World

A. Finding the Main Idea
1. **M**   2. **N**   3. **B**

B. Recalling Facts
1. **c**   2. **b**   3. **b**   4. **c**   5. **a**

C. Making Inferences
1. **C**   2. **C**   3. **C**   4. **F**   5. **F**

D. Using Words Precisely
1. a. **S**   b. **A**   c. **O**
2. a. **O**   b. **S**   c. **A**
3. a. **A**   b. **O**   c. **S**
4. a. **A**   b. **S**   c. **O**
5. a. **A**   b. **S**   c. **O**

9 Raoul Wallenberg:
Cheating the Death Machine

A. Finding the Main Idea
1. **B**   2. **N**   3. **M**

B. Recalling Facts
1. **a**   2. **c**   3. **b**   4. **c**   5. **b**

C. Making Inferences
1. **F**   2. **F**   3. **C**   4. **F**   5. **C**

D. Using Words Precisely
1. a. **A**   b. **O**   c. **S**
2. a. **S**   b. **A**   c. **O**
3. a. **O**   b. **A**   c. **S**
4. a. **O**   b. **A**   c. **S**
5. a. **S**   b. **O**   c. **A**

10 Anne and Charles Lindbergh:
Opening the Skies

A. Finding the Main Idea
1. **N**   2. **B**   3. **M**

B. Recalling Facts
1. **c**   2. **a**   3. **a**   4. **b**   5. **b**

C. Making Inferences
1. **C**   2. **F**   3. **F**   4. **C**   5. **F**

D. Using Words Precisely
1. a. **A**   b. **O**   c. **S**
2. a. **S**   b. **A**   c. **O**
3. a. **O**   b. **S**   c. **A**
4. a. **S**   b. **O**   c. **A**
5. a. **A**   b. **S**   c. **O**

11 Yoni Netanyahu:
The Impossible Rescue

A. Finding the Main Idea
1. **M**   2. **N**   3. **B**

B. Recalling Facts
1. **a**   2. **c**   3. **c**   4. **b**   5. **b**

C. Making Inferences
1. **C**   2. **C**   3. **C**   4. **F**   5. **F**

D. Using Words Precisely
1. a. **O**   b. **S**   c. **A**
2. a. **A**   b. **O**   c. **S**
3. a. **O**   b. **S**   c. **A**
4. a. **A**   b. **O**   c. **S**
5. a. **S**   b. **A**   c. **O**

12 Steve Biko:
South African Freedom Fighter

A. Finding the Main Idea
1. **B**   2. **N**   3. **M**

B. Recalling Facts
1. **b**   2. **a**   3. **c**   4. **c**   5. **b**

C. Making Inferences
1. **F**   2. **F**   3. **C**   4. **F**   5. **C**

D. Using Words Precisely
1. a. **A**   b. **O**   c. **S**
2. a. **S**   b. **O**   c. **A**
3. a. **A**   b. **S**   c. **O**
4. a. **O**   b. **S**   c. **A**
5. a. **S**   b. **O**   c. **A**

13 The Little Rock Nine

A. Finding the Main Idea
1. **M**   2. **N**   3. **B**

B. Recalling Facts
1. **c**   2. **c**   3. **b**   4. **a**   5. **b**

C. Making Inferences
1. **F**   2. **C**   3. **C**   4. **F**   5. **F**

D. Using Words Precisely
1. a. **S**   b. **A**   c. **O**
2. a. **O**   b. **A**   c. **S**
3. a. **S**   b. **O**   c. **A**
4. a. **A**   b. **S**   c. **O**
5. a. **S**   b. **O**   c. **A**

14 Richard Hughes and the Dust of Life

A. Finding the Main Idea
1. **N**   2. **B**   3. **M**

B. Recalling Facts
1. **c**   2. **c**   3. **a**   4. **c**   5. **b**

C. Making Inferences
1. **C**   2. **F**   3. **C**   4. **F**   5. **F**

D. Using Words Precisely
1. a. **S**   b. **O**   c. **A**
2. a. **A**   b. **S**   c. **O**
3. a. **O**   b. **S**   c. **A**
4. a. **A**   b. **O**   c. **S**
5. a. **S**   b. **A**   c. **O**

15 Roberto Clemente: A Duty to Others

A. Finding the Main Idea
1. N   2. B   3. M

B. Recalling Facts
1. b   2. c   3. b   4. a   5. c

C. Making Inferences
1. F   2. F   3. C   4. F   5. F

D. Using Words Precisely
1. a. A   b. O   c. S
2. a. S   b. A   c. O
3. a. A   b. S   c. O
4. a. S   b. A   c. O
5. a. O   b. S   c. A

16 Frank Serpico: An Honest Cop

A. Finding the Main Idea
1. B   2. N   3. M

B. Recalling Facts
1. b   2. a   3. a   4. b   5. c

C. Making Inferences
1. C   2. F   3. F   4. F   5. C

D. Using Words Precisely
1. a. S   b. A   c. O
2. a. A   b. O   c. S
3. a. O   b. S   c. A
4. a. O   b. S   c. A
5. a. O   b. S   c. A

17 Nellie Bly: Exposing the Truth

A. Finding the Main Idea
1. N   2. M   3. B

B. Recalling Facts
1. b   2. b   3. b   4. a   5. c

C. Making Inferences
1. C   2. C   3. C   4. F   5. F

D. Using Words Precisely
1. a. S   b. A   c. O
2. a. S   b. O   c. A
3. a. A   b. O   c. S
4. a. S   b. O   c. A
5. a. A   b. O   c. S

18 The Canadian Embassy: A Risk for Friendship

A. Finding the Main Idea
1. B   2. M   3. N

B. Recalling Facts
1. b   2. a   3. a   4. c   5. a

C. Making Inferences
1. C   2. C   3. F   4. C   5. F

D. Using Words Precisely
1. a. O   b. A   c. S
2. a. S   b. A   c. O
3. a. O   b. S   c. A
4. a. A   b. S   c. O
5. a. S   b. O   c. A

19 Florence Nightingale: A Mission for Life

A. Finding the Main Idea
1. N   2. B   3. M

B. Recalling Facts
1. b   2. c   3. c   4. a   5. b

C. Making Inferences
1. C   2. C   3. F   4. F   5. C

D. Using Words Precisely
1. a. A   b. S   c. O
2. a. A   b. O   c. S
3. a. O   b. A   c. S
4. a. S   b. A   c. O
5. a. S   b. A   c. O

20 James Bond Stockdale: Prisoner of War

A. Finding the Main Idea
1. B   2. N   3. M

B. Recalling Facts
1. c   2. c   3. b   4. b   5. c

C. Making Inferences
1. C   2. F   3. F   4. F   5. C

D. Using Words Precisely
1. a. A   b. S   c. O
2. a. S   b. A   c. O
3. a. S   b. O   c. A
4. a. A   b. O   c. S
5. a. S   b. A   c. O

21 Hans and Sophie Scholl: Resisting Nazi Terror

A. Finding the Main Idea
1. N   2. B   3. M

B. Recalling Facts
1. a   2. b   3. c   4. a   5. c

C. Making Inferences
1. F   2. F   3. F   4. C   5. C

D. Using Words Precisely
1. a. S   b. A   c. O
2. a. S   b. O   c. A
3. a. O   b. A   c. S
4. a. A   b. O   c. S
5. a. S   b. O   c. A

WORDS PER MINUTE TABLE
& PROGRESS GRAPHS

Words per Minute

Unit ▶	Sample	1	2	3	4	5	6	7	
No. of Words ▶	858	1105	920	1254	1531	1370	976	1334	
1:30	572	737	613	836	1021	913	651	889	90
1:40	515	663	552	752	919	822	586	800	100
1:50	468	603	502	684	835	747	532	728	110
2:00	429	552	460	627	765	685	488	667	120
2:10	396	510	425	579	707	632	450	616	130
2:20	368	474	394	537	656	587	418	572	140
2:30	343	442	368	502	612	548	390	534	150
2:40	322	414	345	470	574	514	366	500	160
2:50	303	390	325	443	540	484	344	471	170
3:00	286	368	307	418	510	457	325	445	180
3:10	271	349	291	396	483	433	308	421	190
3:20	257	332	276	376	459	411	293	400	200
3:30	245	316	263	358	437	391	279	381	210
3:40	234	301	251	342	418	374	266	364	220
3:50	224	288	240	327	399	357	255	348	230
4:00	215	276	230	314	383	342	245	333	240
4:10	206	265	221	301	367	329	234	320	250
4:20	198	255	212	289	353	316	225	308	260
4:30	191	246	204	279	340	304	217	296	270
4:40	184	237	197	269	328	294	209	286	280
4:50	178	229	190	259	317	283	202	276	290
5:00	172	221	184	251	306	274	195	267	300
5:10	166	214	178	243	296	265	189	258	310
5:20	161	207	173	235	287	257	183	250	320
5:30	156	201	167	228	278	249	177	243	330
5:40	151	195	162	221	270	242	172	235	340
5:50	147	189	158	215	262	235	167	229	350
6:00	143	184	153	209	255	228	163	222	360
6:10	139	179	149	203	248	222	158	216	370
6:20	135	174	145	198	242	216	154	211	380
6:30	132	170	142	193	236	211	150	205	390
6:40	129	166	138	188	230	206	146	200	400
6:50	126	162	135	184	224	200	143	195	410
7:00	123	158	131	179	219	196	139	191	420
7:20	117	151	125	171	209	187	133	182	440
7:40	112	144	120	164	200	179	127	174	460
8:00	107	138	115	157	191	171	122	167	480

Minutes and Seconds ▶

Seconds ◀

154

GROUP TWO

Unit ▶	8	9	10	11	12	13	14	
No. of Words ▶	1367	1384	1403	1122	1350	1164	1106	
1:30	911	923	935	748	900	776	737	90
1:40	820	830	842	673	810	698	664	100
1:50	746	755	765	612	736	635	603	110
2:00	683	692	701	561	675	582	553	120
2:10	631	639	648	518	623	537	510	130
2:20	586	593	601	481	579	499	474	140
2:30	547	554	561	489	540	466	442	150
2:40	513	519	526	421	506	437	415	160
2:50	482	488	495	396	476	411	390	170
3:00	456	461	468	374	450	388	369	180
3:10	432	437	443	354	426	368	349	190
3:20	410	415	420	337	405	349	332	200
3:30	391	395	401	321	386	333	316	210
3:40	373	377	383	306	368	317	302	220
3:50	357	361	366	293	352	304	289	230
4:00	342	346	351	281	338	291	276	240
4:10	328	332	337	269	324	279	265	250
4:20	315	319	324	259	312	269	255	260
4:30	304	308	312	249	300	259	246	270
4:40	293	297	301	240	289	249	237	280
4:50	283	286	290	232	279	241	229	290
5:00	273	277	281	224	270	233	221	300
5:10	265	268	272	217	261	225	214	310
5:20	256	260	263	210	253	218	207	320
5:30	249	252	255	204	245	212	201	330
5:40	241	244	248	198	238	205	195	340
5:50	234	237	241	192	231	200	190	350
6:00	228	231	234	190	225	194	184	360
6:10	222	224	228	182	219	189	179	370
6:20	216	219	222	177	213	184	175	380
6:30	210	213	216	173	208	179	170	390
6:40	205	208	210	168	203	175	166	400
6:50	200	203	205	164	198	170	162	410
7:00	195	198	200	160	193	166	158	420
7:20	186	189	191	153	184	159	151	440
7:40	178	181	183	146	176	152	144	460
8:00	171	173	175	140	169	146	138	480

Minutes and Seconds (left) — *Seconds* (right)

GROUP THREE

Unit ▶	15	16	17	18	19	20	21	
No. of Words ▶	1103	1354	1021	1039	1260	1284	1274	
1:30	735	903	681	693	840	856	849	90
1:40	662	812	613	623	756	770	764	100
1:50	602	739	557	567	687	700	695	110
2:00	551	677	510	519	630	642	637	120
2:10	509	625	471	480	582	593	588	130
2:20	473	580	438	445	540	550	546	140
2:30	441	542	408	416	504	514	510	150
2:40	414	508	383	390	473	482	478	160
2:50	389	478	360	367	445	453	450	170
3:00	368	451	340	346	420	428	425	180
3:10	348	428	322	328	398	405	402	190
3:20	331	406	306	311	378	385	382	200
3:30	315	387	292	297	360	367	364	210
3:40	301	369	278	283	344	350	347	220
3:50	288	353	266	271	329	335	332	230
4:00	276	338	255	260	315	321	318	240
4:10	265	325	245	249	302	308	306	250
4:20	255	312	236	240	291	296	294	260
4:30	245	301	227	231	280	285	283	270
4:40	236	290	219	223	270	275	273	280
4:50	228	280	211	215	261	266	264	290
5:00	221	271	204	208	252	257	255	300
5:10	213	262	198	201	244	249	247	310
5:20	207	254	191	195	236	241	239	320
5:30	201	246	186	189	229	233	232	330
5:40	195	239	180	183	222	227	225	340
5:50	189	232	175	178	216	220	218	350
6:00	184	226	170	173	210	214	212	360
6:10	179	220	166	168	204	208	207	370
6:20	174	214	161	164	199	203	201	380
6:30	170	208	157	160	194	198	196	390
6:40	165	203	153	156	189	192	191	400
6:50	161	198	149	152	184	188	186	410
7:00	158	193	146	148	180	183	182	420
7:20	150	185	139	142	172	175	174	440
7:40	144	177	133	136	164	167	166	460
8:00	138	169	128	130	158	161	159	480

Minutes and Seconds (left) — *Seconds* (right)

Reading Speed

Directions: *Write your Words per Minute score for each unit in the box under the number of the unit. Then plot your reading speed on the graph by putting a small* **x** *on the line directly above the number of the unit, across from the number of words per minute you read. As you mark your speed for each unit, graph your progress by drawing a line to connect the* **x**'s.

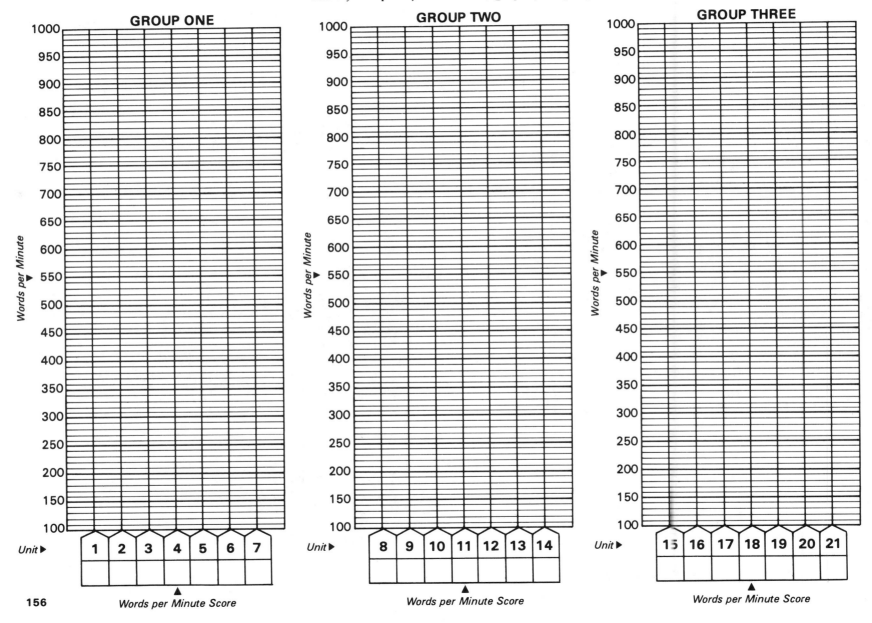

GROUP ONE

Words per Minute

| Unit ► | 1 | 2 | 3 | 4 | 5 | 6 | 7 |

Words per Minute Score

GROUP TWO

Words per Minute

| Unit ► | 8 | 9 | 10 | 11 | 12 | 13 | 14 |

Words per Minute Score

GROUP THREE

Words per Minute

| Unit ► | 15 | 16 | 17 | 18 | 19 | 20 | 21 |

Words per Minute Score

156

Critical Reading Scores

Directions: *Write your Critical Reading Score for each unit in the box under the number of the unit. Then plot your score on the graph by putting a small* **x** *on the line directly above the number of the unit, across from the score you earned. As you mark your score for each unit, graph your progress by drawing a line to connect the* **x**'s.

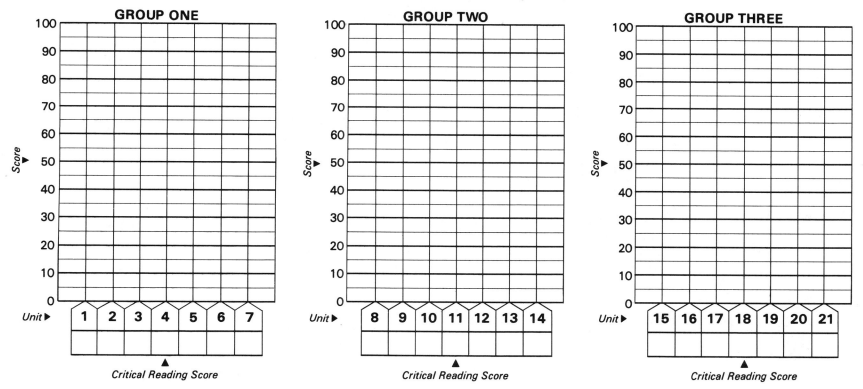

Picture Credits